HOW H

Heart of the
NORFOLK BROADS

David Holmes

Published by the

How Hill Trust

Ludham
Great Yarmouth Norfolk
2011

Contents

Mike Page's superb view of How Hill House from the air.

Author's Note

The foreword and first five sections of this book appeared as 'The How Hill Story', published by the How Hill Trust in 1988. This slim volume has been long out-of-print, and much has happened since its appearance. I have therefore taken this opportunity to revise those sections and to add a sixth, representing a highly personal review of the last 23 years. The second half of this book is a collection of essays on aspects of How Hill and the Broads. The colour sections and many of the other photographs are published here for the first time. Photographic credits appear at the end of the book.

I owe a huge debt of gratitude to my wife Sue, not only for her unwavering support through many challenging years at How Hill, but also for typing much of the text of this book. As Centre Manager for the How Hill Trust for many years she did so much to build up this unique enterprise and, when she retired at the end of 2010, she proved to be irreplaceable. My niece Charlotte Broom, also a familiar face at How Hill events, typed much of the second half of this work. I cannot begin to list those who supported Sue and I in the unending campaign to keep How Hill alive, but I feel that I should note my real and lasting gratitude to Nigel Hill, Chairman of the How Hill Steering Committee, and for many years Clerk to the Trustees, and to Keith McDougall and his successors as Chairman of Trustees, Jonathan Peel CBE and Nick Price FRICS. Others who have had the unenviable task of encouraging me in this enterprise have included Standley Bushell, Iain Mawson, Tim O'Riordan, Peter Sharman, Tom Shephard, and the late, and much missed, Aitken Clark.

Many of my younger teaching colleagues at How Hill have not stayed long, gaining employment at other Centres, in schools, or in other environmental projects, underlining the role of the Trust as a key training ground for education staff. Amongst those who have made a lasting impact I would include Simon Partridge, Vic Stares, Emily Goldsmith, Julia Bustin and Martin McDonnell. The current quartet of Shauna McDougall, Emily Martin, Elanor Nicholls and Katherine Paul are also first class and represent a real and continuing asset to the Trust.

I suppose it may be unfair to mention the names of some of the catering and outside staff without listing them all, but I cannot omit Chris Tubby, the Trust's gardener since 2007, who has restored the gardens into an undoubted treasure for all our visitors. Neither can I leave out Mrs Ruby Edwards, who worked in the How Hill kitchens in the County Council days and has only recently retired. Her more famous husband Eric Edwards MBE, has found part-time work with the Trust after around 40 years in the How Hill marshes, and his love for How Hill is legendary. When, at a recent meeting of retired Norfolk headteachers, he was asked if he thought How Hill was the best place in Norfolk, he replied "it is the only place".

David Holmes
How Hill Trust, Ludham.

"The White House" at How Hill is almost ready for its first occupants, 1905.

Foreword

Broadland is a wonderful complex of natural habitats, each created by man. It is this unique blend of social and natural history which creates the special magic of the area. How Hill, a house and estate set in the heart of this region, represents Broadland in miniature. Winter still sees the traditional reed harvest at How Hill. In June, swallowtail butterflies still beat their way across the fen, and marsh harriers still quarter the reed-beds, plunging suddenly to catch food for their young. In summer the marshman scythes his way through the sedge-beds, and in autumn the teal and wigeon return from their northerly breeding grounds, whilst the newly fledged redshank fly to the coast. Man and nature still work in harmony at How Hill, despite centuries of change, and the rhythm of the seasons still rules.

The How Hill Corn Windmill, at the end of the nineteenth century, before E T Boardman's alterations.

PART ONE : A HISTORY OF HOW HILL

1 Origins

At the beginning of the twentieth century How Hill was discovered by E. T. Boardman, and its remarkable story began to be recorded, in photographs, letters and family documents. But the earlier history of How Hill is vague and sketchy, and awaits detailed research. Speculation can help to disperse the mists of time, guided in part by a few significant facts.

The glacial origin of the hill is clear enough – it represents a knoll of sand and gravel laid down as outwash from a melting ice-sheet, a remnant of a much larger plateau, which was comprehensively eroded by glacial meltwaters as the ice retreated at the end of the Ice Age. Considerably later, the low areas around the hill underwent a series of changes of height relative to the sea. In the two centuries following 2000 BC there was a marine transgression, turning the low areas into a tidal estuary, and this produced a layer of clay. After this, marshland vegetation gradually emerged, and, as the sea level dropped progressively, woodland vegetation began to develop. Eventually this phase produced a thick layer of brushwood peat, and this too was covered with clay resulting from an advance of the sea, some time after 500 BC. A further complex of marshland developed, laying down another layer of peat, and slowly the relative sea level dropped again.

Invaders from Denmark started to land in East Anglia by 865 AD, and their longships penetrated the 'Great Estuary' of Broadland. Their particular legacy is the profusion of Scandinavian place names, such as Filby and Ormesby; How Hill owes its name to these settlers. Previously spelt as Haugr or Haugh Hill, it simply meant a hill surrounded by marshy meadows. How tempting it is to speculate on the importance of this prominent site for the invading Danes. Only a little imagination conjures the prow of a beached longship at a shallow staithe (itself a Danish word), with its blond, helmeted crew plotting some new territorial expansion from the viewpoint of the hill, commanding a prospect of their new-found land.

The Danes and the Angles made some sort of peace in east Norfolk, and gradually the two cultures blended, only to be subjugated by the Norman lords and monks after the conquest. In early medieval times the sea level was lower than it is today, perhaps by as much as thirteen feet. This relative dryness of the marshland provided suitable conditions for peat-digging, and large quantities of this low grade fuel were extracted for domestic use and for sale. Production of peat (known as 'turbary') is recorded in the parish of Ludham in 1383, and this probably refers to the plot of land which later became Crome's Broad, at How Hill. At this time the peat cutting was taxed by means of tithes paid to St Benet's Abbey, and we shall probably never know when the peat cutting became flooded to form a Broad. Water levels started to rise in the late thirteenth century, but the Ant Valley Broads were amongst the last to form.

The Wherry '*Dispatch*' sailing past How Hill Staithe with her skipper George Rump at the helm, 1936.

The medieval Broadland must have been an unhealthy, difficult environment, but nonetheless magical to anyone who had the leisure to enjoy it. Bitterns were abundant, and it seems that cranes, black terns, spoonbills, black tailed godwits, and perhaps even glossy ibises bred in the marshes. Toad Hole Cottage was built by the river at How Hill in the eighteenth century, but there was certainly a dwelling on this site in much earlier times, and the marshmen probably lived in much the same way as that described by Richard Lubbock in 1845 ... "life presented no vicissitudes but an alternation of marsh employment. In winter, after his day's reed cutting, he might be regularly found posted at nightfall, waiting for the flight of fowl or paddling after them on the open water". At all seasons, there was a harvest to be taken from the river or the marsh, and the marshman's family would never have starved. In Victorian times, the demand for eels in East London provided the cottage occupants with a regular income, and eels were trapped in thousands using an eel sett stretched across the river.

An early picture postcard of How Hill Staithe with a well laden wherry drifting by.

At the end of the eighteenth century the old way of life must have started to change. Wherry transport was in its heyday, and the waterways of the Broads were deepened, widened and straightened. At How Hill, the river Ant once meandered around the far western border of the present estate, but by 1797 the maps show its present course. Who organised and paid for the cutting of the new channel? How many men were engaged in the process, and how long did it take? How was the work undertaken?

In 1802 the land at How Hill was 'enclosed' and the enclosure Act gives details of the new fields and plots, and of ownership. In 1825 a brick tower mill was built at the top of the hill, by William Sherwood Page, who let both the mill and the mill house in 1831. The Page family owned farmland at How Hill, as well as marsh pasture alongside the Ant, but seemed to prefer to let the land to tenant farmers. At this time How Hill Staithe was established, for wherries to unload corn for the miller, or to load the sacks of flour, and the lane up to the mill became wide enough for carts.

In 1865 Walter White published a two volume work on 'Eastern England', recounting his travels in the summer of 1860. Volume One provides one of the earliest references to "How Hill, a big knoll, thickly covered with oat grass, from the top of which we had a pleasant view, and enjoyed the scent of elder blossom with which we had become familiar; broad reedy flats, pastures of various colour, coarse swamps, bright patches of poppies, irregular patches of water, windmills and dykes, and the narrow stream repeating its lazy curves across the vast level".

White noted that those left aboard his chartered yacht on the river Ant could hear every word of his conversation with a fellow traveller at the summit of How Hill, a quarter of a mile away; in certain conditions this is still possible.

At the end of the nineteenth century the Page family was still in possession of How Hill, and their tenant farmer regularly dug sand and gravel from the hill for the tracks and farmyard. A shallow gravel pit shows up on the earliest photographs of the site. The last of the How Hill eel catchers, Ben Curtis, was still living in Toad Hole Cottage, but he moved out at about the turn of the century. The scene was set for the arrival of the Boardman family, whose first purchase at Ludham was of about 190 acres including the hill, the mill, by now disused, the millhouse, and farmland down to the river.

2 The Boardman Family and the Holiday Home

How Hill's story is also the story of the Boardman family, and in particular it is the story of its owner and architect, Edward Thomas Boardman. His father, Edward Boardman, founded the family firm of architects in 1860, at the age of twenty-seven, and a year later Edward Thomas was born. He joined his father in the firm in 1889, and became head of the firm on his father's retirement in 1900. Because of the similarity of names, it is necessary to observe the family convention of referring to the father as Edward and the son as Edward Thomas. During the last forty years of the nineteenth century, Boardman and Son, of Queen Street, Norwich, became the most influential firm of architects in the city, and their work can still be seen today.

Most notable amongst the Boardman projects of this period were the redevelopment of London Street (1876–80), the building of the Norfolk and Norwich Hospital (1879–83), and the conversion of Norwich Castle into a museum. The idea of converting Norwich gaol into a museum was Edward Boardman's, and in 1885 he embarked on a campaign to convince J. H. Gurney and other eminent citizens of the value of such a scheme. Mr Gurney was very resistant to the idea at first, but in reply to his remark that the buildings were "too cracked about and utterly unfit for the purpose", Mr Boardman asserted that "if they will hold prisoners they will hold dead birds". Eventually he prepared a three dimensional model of his scheme so that Mr Gurney, who was blind, might be convinced. Clearly, he was convinced, because he subscribed £5,000 to the project, and the building was purchased from the government, converted and fitted out, and opened to the public in 1894.

Edward Boardman was a prominent citizen of Norwich. He was elected to the City Council in 1889, and accepted the much-respected position of Alderman in 1898. He was for many years a Deacon of the Princes Street Congregational Church which had been rebuilt to his designs in 1868–69. This Church exerted a major role in Norwich society, since so many important citizens worshipped there, including all the senior members of the Colman family. Edward Boardman was a deeply religious man, and was held in high regard on all sides.

It was against such a background of success and influence that the young Edward Thomas Boardman joined his father's firm. In addition to professional training during four years articled to his father, Edward Thomas had also spent two years in the offices of Ernest George and Peto, eminent London architects, and had studied architecture at University College London and at the associated Slade School of Fine Art. He had also travelled considerably, visiting Holland, Belgium, Germany, Morocco, Spain, India and Italy. Thus he was ably equipped to further the work of the practice, and together with their chief surveyor, C. W. Yelf, and chief draughtsman Graham Cotman, father and son were able to extend the Boardman dominance in architecture in Norwich and the county.

They worked for most of the major industrial firms in Norwich, designing factories, warehouses, and shops for Caley's, Page Bros., Chamberlins, Harmers, Howlett & Whites, the Norfolk News Company, and Laurence Scott and Company. They worked for Barclays and for the Norwich Union Fire Insurance Society. In the county, eminent families seeking to modernise and extend their country homes naturally sought help from Boardman and Son: the halls at Hardingham, Bagthorpe, Oulton, Bolwick, and Kilverstone are all in this category. A good many public houses were Boardman designed, as the firm were for many years architects to the brewery, Youngs, Crawshaw and Youngs.

It is difficult to identify which buildings were solely the work of Edward Thomas, and which were jointly supervised with his father. It is known however that the 'Leicester' Nurses Home (in Norwich) was primarily designed by Edward Thomas, as was Cromer Hospital, the Royal Hotel, Norwich (1896-98), and that he worked on cottages and the village hall at Scarning, taking his instructions from the author Dr Augustus Jessop. He also worked on Crown Point Hall (which became Whitlingham Hospital), and designed a splendid range of stables and outbuildings at Kilverstone Hall. One of his most celebrated buildings, Gurney's Bank (Barclays) in Bank Plain, Norwich, was in fact a joint project with Brierley and Rutherford of York (1929-31). A major commission for the Norwich Cooperative Society, a new "machine bakery" (1913), is one of several Boardman buildings which are now 'listed'. Some of his smaller Norwich buildings were important in their own way: Stuart Court, in Recorder Road, a development of flats for the old and needy of Norwich (1915), was commissioned by Helen Colman, who had been very concerned about the poor standard of housing in the city. He carried on his father's work as architect for the Norfolk and Norwich Hospital, frequently returning at least part of his fees as a donation.

In 1898 Edward Thomas married Florence Esther Colman, youngest daughter of Jeremiah James Colman, Chairman of the Carrow Works which still ensure that both the Colman family name and the name of Norwich enjoy currency worldwide. He was MP for Norwich (1871-95) and had a large country house at The Clyffe, Corton, on the Suffolk coast. Born in 1869, one of Florence Esther's earliest recollections was of staying up one night at Corton so that she might hear her father talking with Mr Gladstone.

Wedding day, 9th September, 1898.

The wedding, on Friday September 9th, 1898, at the Free Methodist Chapel, Corton, was naturally followed by a splendid social gathering at The Clyffe, but the bride and groom started the day rather less formally. Florence bathed in the sea with her dogs, whilst Edward Thomas was sailing round from Lowestoft. On arrival, he beached his boat and waded ashore, but presented himself in full formal attire at the service at 2 p.m. The new Mrs Boardman had four young bridesmaids and two page boys (Geoffrey Colman and Tristan D'Oyly), the sun shone and the band played. A pony and trap took the newlyweds, and dogs, to the station, and the honeymoon was spent at Calthorpe, a small Broadland estate not far from Hickling.

The couple made their home at Town Close House, Ipswich Road, Norwich, rented from the estate trustees. The rent was low, but it was expected that tenants should maintain and improve the property at their own expense, which Mr Boardman was happy to do, adding a new drive and extensions in due course. One of their summer holidays proved to be especially significant. The couple planned to spend a fortnight on the Broads (probably in 1901) and hired the pleasure wherry '*Gaviota*' to meet them at Wroxham. They reached the riverside with provisions and luggage, and it started to rain – but there was no sign of the '*Gaviota*'. A friendly wherryman offered shelter on his trading wherry, the '*John Henry*'. This vessel carried cargo in the winter but was used for cruising in summer.. It certainly was not as well fitted as the wherry the couple had expected, and – significantly – it was a good deal smaller. They later found out that the booking for '*Gaviota*' had gone astray, and she was sailing on the Waveney, but the John Henry took them up the River Ant to Stalham – passing under the old humpbacked Ludham bridge, which the '*Gaviota*' could never have done. They thus saw How Hill, or Haugh Hill as it was spelt on older maps, and spotted its potential as a site for their new holiday home.

Mr & Mrs Edward Boardman, with Joan, the twins Humphrey and Stuart, and Christopher, 1905.

1902 was a busy year. On January 14th Mrs Boardman had her first child, Joan Caroline, and Nanny Rolfe was recruited to look after her. Mr Boardman meanwhile negotiated to buy the estate at How Hill. Included in his initial purchase was the Mill House and the derelict tower windmill, and half of Crome's Broad. Later he was able to acquire the remainder of Crome's Broad, and more land, until the estate covered 872 acres. The Mill House provided excellent accommodation for the family's first visits to How Hill, but Mr Boardman began thinking about his new house, and decided to have it pure white, with coloured decoration, and with all bedroom and living room windows facing south.

Christopher Alan Boardman was born on June 11th 1903, and the plans of the new house bear the date October 25th 1903. The house had sitting room, hall, dining room, kitchen, servants hall and a range of utility rooms on the ground floor, with stairs to a master bedroom, night nursery and day nursery on the first floor, and three more bedrooms on the second floor. The architectural details of window casements, door handles and latches, and of decoration on chimneys and around windows, were all carefully drawn out by Mr Boardman, and he kept a very close watch on progress. However, the intricate wood carvings which still decorate the door surrounds in the entrance hall, were the work of his sister, Ethel (later to become Mrs Percy Jewson). The date over the front door is 1904, but photographs show that the house was not ready for occupation until April 1905.

Joan, Christopher and the twins, 1905.

In the meantime the twins were born (July 26th 1904) – Humphrey Colman Boardman and Stuart Cozens-Hardy Boardman, named in honour of their mother's eminent relatives. Florence Cork was recruited as nanny for the twins, and thus began a lifetime of service with the family. Because she shared the same Christian name as Mrs Boardman, she had to be given a less confusing name, and was called Corky, for nearly half a century. The two eldest children were taken to the launch of the wherry '*Hathor*' at Reedham in July 1905. The wherry was commissioned by Mrs Boardman's two sisters, Helen and Ethel Colman, and was named after the vessel on which their brother Alan had died in Egypt, eight years earlier. Edward Thomas had supervised the

Walter Woolston, Gamekeeper at How Hill.

construction of the wherry, and he designed the remarkable Egyptian interior: it was his children who stole the show at the launch. Joan performed the most charming part of the ceremony, opening a wicker basket to set free some pigeons, to the delight of her aunts and their guests.

By this time Edward Thomas had become a prominent citizen of Norwich. He was elected to the City Council in 1899, as member for Town Close ward, and he held this seat for twenty years. In November 1905 he became Mayor of the City (four years later the title became Lord Mayor, and Mr Boardman later became the last surviving holder of the earlier office). He served on several committees, and was Chairman of the City Higher Education Committee, during which time the City of Norwich School was opened. He was very concerned with education, advancing the cause of technical education and establishing the Boardman Scholarship for architectural students. He was a Justice of the Peace, and an advocate for public parks and gardens in the city: he was a prime mover in the city's purchase of Eaton Park. He was founder president of the Norfolk and Norwich Association of Architects, was a Trustee of the East Anglian Trustee Savings Bank, and later, was President of the Norfolk and Norwich Naturalists' Society. Another of his public interests was in the relief of unemployment, and in 1906 he established a scheme for the unemployed to emigrate to Canada where jobs were available. In furtherance of this scheme he made a visit to Canada.

Left to right: Humphrey, Joan, Stuart, Christopher Boardman.

Throughout the period up to the First World War, How Hill was the 'holiday home'. Guardians of the estate whilst the family was in Norwich were the Woolstons, who lived in the Mill House. Walter Woolston had been gamekeeper at Calthorpe, but after the death of his employer (Mrs Boardman's brother Alan Colman) he was offered work at How Hill. He was, by all accounts, a marvellous man, full of wisdom about the wildlife and traditions of the Broads, and ever willing both to play with, and to educate, the Boardman children. The family albums are full of pictures of the white-bearded Woolston explaining the secrets of natural history to the youngsters, or letting them climb on to him to play "horses", or simply nursing them in the back of a punt.

Mrs Boardman was busy building up the kitchen garden. The family would arrive by horse and trap, having used the ferry at Horning as a short-cut, and she would immediately inspect the turkeys and chickens, and her vegetables, near the Mill House. Her husband was busy planting trees (70,000 in all) and developing the two gardens. The yew hedges were laid out, together with borders and rose gardens. A new thatched boat house was added at the staithe, and a sluice gate built on the dyke leading to the Broad. A single storey flat roofed sun room was added to the house in 1910, and the entrance was altered so that vehicles (and passers-by) could no longer come to the front door.

Happy family days at How Hill staithe.

On October 11th 1910 the Boardman family gathered at Cliffside, Overstrand, to celebrate the golden wedding of Edward and Martha Boardman. Edward Thomas took his wife and their two eldest children to the celebration. A massive silver salver was the main present to the couple from the family, and this was engraved with all their names. Telegrams were read out from the staff of the firm and from the Liberal Club in Norwich. Exactly a month later Edward Boardman died; Edward Thomas and Florence attended the funeral at The Rosary, Norwich, and an era in both family and city history came to a close.

The Ant Valley flooded, August 1912.

In the decade before the First World War the marshes at How Hill began to change character. Throughout the nineteenth century the marshes which were not suitable for reeds were either grazed or were mown for marsh litter. Two drainage windmills, which still stand at How Hill, kept a major part of the estate dry enough for summer grazing of beef cattle. On the west bank of the river, the brick built Turf Fen windmill (built in the 1880s) was an efficient structure with two paddle wheels pumping water into the river. This 'double scoop' arrangement is very rare, and perhaps unique in Broadland. On the other side of the river the trestle smock mill, a small wooden structure, drained the 27 acres of Clayrack marshes. It was one of a remarkable group of about 30 Broadland and drainage pumps built by Ludham millwright Dan England. In later years England improved the mechanism of this pump, by installing a turbine which was rather more efficient in lifting the water from the dyke to the river. There was also an older drainage pump at the staithe which Mr Boardman had encased in a conical wooden structure. This was occasionally connected to a steam machine from the farm to take over the pumping on windless days.

The floods of August 1912.

The marshes which were mown provided a rough mixture of grass, sedge and rushes which was used for animal feedstuffs or stable bedding; a great deal of the Broadland marsh litter was sent to London, but from about 1910 the horse drawn vehicles were rapidly replaced with mechanical wagons and 'horseless carriages'. The marshes, no longer mown, became overgrown with scrub; no longer pumped, reverted to reed swamp, and the landscape changed. A contributory factor was the flood of August 1912, which damaged sluices, pumps and bridges; but for a few days provided the Boardman children with an exciting change of scenery. Seven inches of rain fell in a day, causing widespread dislocation and damage in East Anglia, as well as a ruined harvest, but the sunshine which followed over the next week or so glistened on a magical temporary waterscape in the Ant Valley.

The twins initiate Freshwater Ecology studies at How Hill.

The Boardman children had a wonderful time on their visits to How Hill. They spent a lot of time at the staithe, paddling and, later, swimming, always with a nanny or Woolston in attendance. They were taught to sail in a dinghy which Mr Boardman had built for them, called 'Bobs' after the hero Lord Roberts. There was a tarred and weather beaten houseboat which they played on, and a rowing boat called '*Mariner*' which the staff were free to use. Joan and her friends enjoyed the use of Toad Hole, the cottage by the river, and they painted it and wallpapered it, eventually making some of their own meals there and even sleeping there on summer nights. In 1914 Mrs Boardman had another son, Michael Russell, and Joan was old enough to be able to help to nurse the baby.

One of the twins fishing at How Hill Staithe.

During the First World War Mr Boardman worked on new plans for the house. He prepared two alternative proposals, one of which was very grand. At right angles to the existing house, a new wing would be added, offering a bow windowed drawing room, hall, dining room, and a long balcony, all with elevated views over the valley. On the eastern side of the new wing would be a porch, with steps curving away, and a 'business room', together with a rear staircase to bedrooms above, relegating the old stairs to the status of 'back stairs' - the old drawing room would now become the servants hall. The square formed in the right angle between the two wings would become a courtyard. The overall dimensions of the new wing would have been about 94 feet by 30 feet and considerable earth moving would have been required to build up the site. In the event, an alternative plan came to fruition. The sun room would be retained, though modified and enlarged, and above it would be added a large new bedroom and dressing room on the first floor, with three more bedrooms on the second floor. Built at right angles to the main house would be a new semicircular bay composed of twelve curved windows. This magnificent room, 42 feet by 23 feet, was complete with a vaulted ceiling and an alcove fireplace, and underneath it a cosy loggia could be provided as a garden feature.

Thatching the new reception room, 1916.

The extended How Hill House, almost completed.

Christopher sets off with his butterfly net, after the builders had finished their work.

Edward Thomas Boardman with his sons Christopher, Humphrey and Stuart.

The new building work was completed in 1916, despite the difficulties of labour and supply of materials in wartime. And at the end of the war Mr Boardman decided that it was no longer either necessary or practical to keep two houses. With the advance of motor transport, he could work in Norwich and live at How Hill. The war had wrought drastic social and economic changes, and it no longer made sense to maintain two households. In 1918, therefore, How Hill became the Boardman family home.

Turf Fen Drainage Windmill.

3 The Family Home

After the war the children's education took priority, culminating in a naval training for Christopher, at Osborne and Dartmouth, and school for the twins at Malvern followed by Cambridge, where Stuart read agriculture in readiness for taking on the farm, and Humphrey studied architecture, to follow his father into the firm. Edward Thomas commuted to the office in Norwich by motorbike, and whenever possible he would waste no daylight on his return, either playing tennis at Toad Hole, or busying himself in the bog garden. He always worked alongside his men, who included at various times Dan Boulter, Billy Slaughter, George Nudd and Bob Platford. The men took on other miscellaneous tasks as well; Platford looked after the horses, Nudd was a reed cutter, Boulter looked after the cars, and even used to cut the twins' hair.

Edward Thomas Boardman on the terrace at How Hill.

Whilst the twins were at Cambridge, Mrs Boardman encouraged them to bring their friends for house parties at How Hill. In addition to large weekend parties, it was possible for the twins to leave Cambridge at 6 a.m., have breakfast at How Hill, spend the day on the estate, and race back to college for the night, to conform with Cambridge rules. Mrs Boardman was so pleased to see her sons prosper at Cambridge that she took rooms in the town during May week so as to enjoy the undoubted social delights of Varsity life in the early 1920s.

At College, rowing on the Cam had natural attractions for Humphrey, brought up on the Broads, and he represented his country twice. In 1928 he went to the Olympic Games in Amsterdam, where he rowed in the coxless pairs event. In August 1930 he won two gold medals in the British Empire Games in Canada, rowing in both eights and fours. In between were visits to Henley and a trip to Germany with the London Rowing Club. Later Humphrey coached Cambridge boat crews, and the whole eight, with cox and one or two supporters, enjoyed Mrs Boardman's lavish hospitality with the family at How Hill. The Ludham butcher was never surprised to be asked for fillet steak for 20!

Joan arrives for her wedding at Ludham Church, accompanied by her father and one of the ushers, Michael Brown, 24 September, 1930.

Mrs Boardman's family had grown up; strong, healthy, attractive and popular, they enjoyed a full and varied social life. Joan was the first to marry, and in September 1930 she became the wife of lawyer Malcolm Lynde. The service was held in Ludham Church and the guests were received at How Hill, but it was a very windy day: the marquee blew down and many of the decorations were ruined. Nonetheless, it was obviously a very happy day, the biggest and most splendid social occasion the house had yet seen.

Edward Thomas Boardman surveys the flower beds by the front door, which are much reduced in size today. Note the flat-roofed sun parlour in the background.

Stuart had taken over the How Hill farm when the tenant had left it at Michaelmas 1926. By all accounts the farm was then in a pretty poor condition, but with the support of his father, Stuart put the farm on a sound footing. They decided to grow fruit, planting over sixty acres of apples, cherries and pears. The trees were under planted with blackcurrants, gooseberries and strawberries. At this time the farm had a foreman, Mr Bloom, and ten full-time workers, two of whom spent the winter reed-cutting. There were three or four horses for farm work, put out on the grazing marsh at night, together with about a dozen bullocks which were penned in the farmyard in the winter.

The farm also had large numbers of poultry and some pigs. Stuart was one of a small group of farmers who promoted the Norfolk Royal apple, still grown at How Hill today. He joined the pioneering marketing co-operative, Norfolk Fruit Growers, in its early years (becoming a Director in 1935). Stuart married a farmer's daughter, Monica Wells, in Norwich Cathedral in November 1930, with a reception afterwards at Carrow. By 1938, the fruit farm had become a commercial success, and Stuart decided to establish some holly bushes for the Christmas trade – and this unusual crop is still a feature of the How Hill Farm.

Humphrey had joined his father in the firm, having become a fully qualified architect, and in 1934 he married Vera Wilson, whom he had known in Norfolk years before, without taking much notice of her. Now she was reputedly 'one of the prettiest girls in London' and appeared in many West End revues as a 'Cochran girl'. (Vera died in 1969 and Humphrey was fortunate enough to make a second happy marriage, with Isabella Aitken in 1971). Christopher and Michael stayed in the family home, and both remained bachelors for some years. Christopher, having left the Navy, joined the staff of Colmans, and was often away from How Hill whilst he negotiated contracts with farmers and growers throughout East Anglia. Michael, having read law at Cambridge, joined the old established firm of Cozens-Hardy and Jewson, Norwich solicitors.

Vera Wilson at harvest time on the How Hill Farm.

Christopher Boardman achieved a considerable reputation as a sailor, no doubt drawing not only on Broadland experience but also on his years in the Navy. He enjoyed early success crewing in '*Peewit*', owned by Miss Beryl Colman (later Lady Mayhew), a 'Brown Boat' – the affectionate name given to the Broads One Design, a famous class of 24 foot wooden yachts which still sail on Oulton Broad and at sea off Lowestoft. He also sailed other Broadland and East Coast craft, including the Brown Boat '*Spoonbill*', and the Yare and Bure One Design '*Clearwing*', as well as his own 14 foot dinghy '*Cayenne*'. Later, he became part-owner of a 6 metre yacht at Burnham-on-Crouch, and then he was asked to join the famous 12 metre yacht '*Shamrock V*' as assistant helmsman. Then came '*Endeavour*', Sir Thomas Sopwith's splendid ocean racer. Sopwith's professional crew went on strike, so Christopher Boardman was asked to sail her, and to find an amateur crew. *Endeavour*, with Christopher and the other 'amateurs' aboard, almost captured the Americas Cup for Britain in 1934.

Christopher Boardman at the helm of *Shamrock V*.

He returned to 6 metre yachts in 1935 and in the following year he took 'Lalage' to Kiel for the 1936 Olympics. He was part-owner of the craft, and as an amateur he had to pay all his own expenses, which were considerable, and had to take time off from his job with Colmans. The Olympics were very different in those days and only 12 nations, mostly European, were represented in the yacht races. Most of the crews had raced each other before, but there were endless protests from some of the more volatile helmsmen, and considerable animosity between some of the crews. In the event, *Lalage* failed to win a single race, but on a points system, and after the disqualification of the Swiss boat, she was awarded the Gold. Christopher later described the result as "farcical"; on his return to England he took his medal into a jewellers, who told him that in fact the Olympic 'gold' was predominantly base metal.

Broads One Designs ('White Boats') racing at Acle Regatta, 31st July 1922, Number 14, '*Clearwing*', skippered by Chris Boardman, in the lead.

Christopher Boardman had neither the time nor the inclination to visit Berlin for the grandiose ceremonies which went with these showpiece Olympics, but his crew member, Miles Belleville, did make the journey, and duly received a little oak sapling from Hitler. The tiny tree was planted at How Hill on September 20th, 1936, by Christopher's friend 'Tiny' Mitchell, Commodore of the Royal Corinthian Yacht Club.

Humphrey and camera at the bittern hide, How Hill, 1926.

Mrs Boardman kept a photographic record of her family, first at Town Close House, and later at How Hill. Her photographs, which she developed herself, provide the basis for any research into the family's history, and she encouraged Humphrey to take up photography. In this he was highly successful, particularly with natural history subjects. His pictures of an adult bittern at her nest were the first ever taken in this country, and were published in 1926, in both the *Eastern Daily Press* and *Country Life*. The nest was only a few yards from the river at How Hill, and he was assisted in his task of hide-building and watching the birds by the celebrated Hickling keeper and naturalist Jim Vincent. Humphrey's picture of a swan taking wing on Hickling Broad achieved even more acclaim, since it formed part of a series showing not only the grace of a swan's flight, but also the method of takeoff. The pictures were published in the *Illustrated London News* (1928) and were discussed in a '*Times*' letter from Sir George Aston.

One of Humphrey Boardman's celebrated pictures of a bittern at the nest,
How Hill, 1926. Note the high water level.

Humphrey's famous photograph of a mute swan taking off at Hickling Broad, 1928.

During the inter-war years the celebrated Yarmouth naturalist, Arthur Patterson, or 'John Knowlittle' as he often called himself, made friends with the Boardman family. Two of his visits to How Hill are recorded in his books. In '*Through Broadland in a Breydon Punt*', published in 1920, Patterson recounts an evening spent with the How Hill gamekeeper, Walter Woolston. They swapped stories of pike and marsh hares. Patterson's description of the old keeper is particularly well-drawn: "I like Woolston: a fine old fellow, a Broadland patriarch with flowing white beard, and a superior manner; his mouth opened guardedly to gossip between the sporran of hair upon his face and chin. I looked at that strong, bearded face again; it reminded me of Aaron's beard depicted in my stepmother's old bible".

Patterson also recorded a 1923 visit to How Hill in '*The Cruise of the Walrus on the Broads*'. He hitched the ropes of his North Sea Ketch to a stump at How Hill staithe and "browned his boots and brushed his hat" before receiving a warm welcome and a civilised lunch with the Boardman family. Afterwards, he noted, "our host and hostess sauntered with us down to the staithe, and bade us God speed, to the accompaniment of a camera's clickings". The resultant photograph is still secure in one of the Boardman family's cherished albums.

Shooting and fishing were always important on the How Hill estate, and the marshes and woods were always managed with this in mind. Nowadays, when shooting is far less popular, attitudes have changed, but the management of game on the How Hill estate undoubtedly preserved other birds and wildlife. When the shooting ceased, the

Arthur Patterson aboard his Ketch "*Walrus*" at How Hill Staithe, 1923.

wildlife interest of the marshes began to diminish, vermin increased and the marshes began to assume a much more derelict appearance. Good shooting required, at How Hill, good conservation. It also required good behaviour, since Michael and Christopher Boardman were very strict about conduct in the field. Considerable effort was expended in picking up all birds shot, and discipline amongst the guns was rigidly demanded. Anyone who verged on unsporting activities was never asked to shoot again.

As with so many Boardman activities, very detailed and accurate records were kept, and the Game Book reads like a 'Who's Who' of shooting. Peter Scott joined the brothers for a shoot in August 1932. Other celebrated guests included Gavin Maxwell, Colin McClean, Douglas McDougall, Meredith Perrin, Alan Savory, The Duke of Grafton, Lt Col. H. J. Cator, Hon. M. Fitzallan Howard, J. C. Harrison (the artist), and Viscount Templewood, not to mention many members of the Colman and Cozens-Hardy families. The game numbers and locations are all faithfully recorded in the Game Book, but the wonderful spirit of How Hill shoots is revealed by observations of birds (particularly of marsh harriers and bitterns) which would certainly never be shot, and by occasional glimpses of light humour. November 30th 1947 carried the entry "Flight of M. Perrin's Purdey into bottom of Broad added interest to the shoot if not numbers to the bag".

Humphrey Boardman's photograph of the Wherry 'Stalham Trader' being quanted past How Hill Staithe, April 1930.

In the early years the shooting at How Hill was all from punts, but later butts were built on wooden posts driven into the marsh. There were four main places for duck 'flighting', that is shooting duck either on their flight into or out of a favoured pool. At How Hill, the naturally flooded Bisley marshes, to the west of the river, provided one morning flight; Crome's Broad provided the other. Two pools on the grazing marsh were used for evening flights. In addition to duck, pheasants, partridges and pigeons were also shot, together with occasional woodcock or snipe. However the record snipe shoot did not occur until much later, 24th November 1962, when there was a sudden thaw after days of hard frost, and the marsh pumps were unexpectedly out of order. Some grazing marsh had recently been ploughed for cereal cropping, and water pushed the earthworms into the surface layer, bringing in the birds. Snipe arrived in thousands, and these exceptional conditions enabled the guns to shoot at snipe driven up by the beaters. The tally was 116, and during the entire season 1962-63, only five other snipe were taken – a day's shooting quite unmatched in How Hill's history.

Members of the Boardman family were amongst the finest shots in the county, and it is not surprising that they were invited to shoot on other estates, particularly Hickling. They joined several of the annual Coot Shoots on the Broad. Christopher and Michael were present at King George VI's last Coot Shoot, on January 31st 1951. The bag on this occasion included 961 coot, but the King had but a year to live, and the great days of shooting were nearly over.

Fishing occupied the brothers at How Hill nearly as much as shooting, although the vast majority of the fish caught were returned to the water. Some superb specimen pike were caught in the Broad, and the record tench which was put straight back after weighing, tipped the

Joan encounters a hazard in the How Hill lane.

scales at 5lb 4oz. Bow nets were used in the dykes, and the numbers of fish finding their way into the nets overnight were phenomenal. Greatest entertainment was provided by various different ways of catching eels, always abundant on summer nights. As Alan Savory noted of How Hill ... "there were hot, still evenings eel-babbing and laying eel-lines when the world seemed to have slipped back a century or two, and there was nothing but the swaying miles of reeds and water and the voices of night birds ...." (Norfolk Fowler, 1953).

In later years a great many duck were caught at How Hill and ringed before release. This has provided a fascinating insight into the migration of mallard and teal from the Broads into distant parts of Europe. For example, four mallard drakes which were ringed consecutively in February 1956 were later found in four separate countries – Denmark (October 1957), Sweden (August 1956), Norway (October 1957) and Germany (August 1956). At least two mallards turned up near Murmansk, and the majority of ringing recoveries were from northern Europe, the Baltic coastlands of Russia, Poland and the Netherlands. Equally interesting were the one or two How Hill ringed birds which were recaptured at the same place in later years.

This picture was published in the magazine 'Autocar' on 19th May 1939, and shows the family's eight cars lined up in front of How Hill.
Left to right:
1. Armstrong Siddeley coupe (Edward Thomas Boardman)
2. Daimler saloon (Mrs Florence Boardman)
3. Ford V8 coupe (Christopher Boardman)
4. Bentley 3 litre (Humphrey Boardman)
5. Morris Eight (Mrs Vera Boardman)
6. Ford v8 saloon (Stuart Boardman)
7. Rover 12 (Michael Boardman)
8. Ford V8 saloon (Malcolm Lynde, Joan's husband)

The Drawing Room, 1928.

The years of the Second World War had been quiet and sober at How Hill by contrast with earlier times. Michael joined the Royal Signals, Humphrey went into the RAF and served in Iraq and Persia, Christopher returned to the Navy and commanded Corvettes in the North Atlantic. Stuart, as a serving officer in the Territorial Reserve, found the village policeman at his farmhouse door on the day war broke out, and was summoned to report for immediate mobilisation. He joined the 5th battalion of the Royal Norfolk Regiment, and reached the rank of Captain before he was killed in action in Malaya in 1942. Joan Lynde, returned to How Hill with her young family whilst her husband was away at war, and she was able to share her mother's grief when the bitter news came through. During the war, a bomb exploded harmlessly on the grazing marshes and a returning German pilot dropped a stick of bombs close to the Mill House. Some of the shrapnel penetrated the main house, but the young 'Hitler's Oak' was unscathed. On one terrifying occasion, How Hill was machine-gunned from the air: fortunately no one was hurt. However, the glow from blazing buildings in Norwich was clearly visible from How Hill after enemy bombing raids on the city.

Florence and Edward read their joint birthday greetings, 2 July 1931.
They shared a birthday: he was 70 and she was 62 on this occasion.

After the war life began to return to normal, but the estate was changing. The farm was kept on but tractors replaced horses and the labour force never returned to pre-war levels, even though more arable land, previously tenanted, was taken in to the farm. The carefree times of gardening, tennis, water sports and marshland adventure at How Hill were gone forever. There were still some grand occasions – on September 9th 1948 there was a lavish party to celebrate Mr and Mrs E. T. Boardman's Golden Wedding, when Lord Cozens-Hardy proposed their health. Edward Thomas was then still active and alert, but on

E T Boardman, with his daughter Joan and workers Mr Nudd (bearded) and
Mr Platford in the How Hill Bog Garden, 1930.

E T Boardman is dwarfed by the
How Hill bamboos, April 1930.

June 16th 1950 he died. He was very nearly 90, a respected Norfolkman and a dearly-loved father. Mrs Boardman lived on at How Hill, determined not to give in to crippling rheumatism, and her sons Michael and Christopher lived in the house with her. She died on July 27th 1960, and the estate was fragmented between the brothers. Christopher inherited the house and the marshland estate, but this provided no income for the upkeep of an increasingly expensive property. He married Elaine Romanine in 1961, and by 1965 they reluctantly decided to put the house and grounds on the market. The Boardman link with How Hill was not severed however, since Stuart's son, Peter, carried on farming at How Hill in partnership with his mother, and Humphrey and Michael continued to maintain land adjoining the River Ant. The Boardman family is still strongly represented in Norfolk, but the architects' firm, by then the oldest in Norwich, was finally dissolved in August 1966.

A postcard view of Turf Fen Drainage Windmill in the inter-war years.

4 The County Residential Education Centre

"The exceptional Broadland residential and sporting estate known as How Hill, extending in all to over 344 acres. A frontage of about 1 mile on each bank to the River Ant. The Principal Residence with 4 reception rooms, 12 bedrooms, 3 bathrooms, gun room, domestic offices, part central heating. Nearly 300 acres of reed and sporting marshes and upland, 30 acres woodland, 2 evening duck-flighting ponds and 2 early morning duck-flighting places, including a private 13 acre Broad. Secondary 4 bedroom Residence, water garden, and 2 cottages."

The advertisement for the sale of How Hill House, from *Country Life* magazine, May 1966.

This was the auctioneer's description of the property on offer in the Royal Hotel, Norwich, on Saturday June 18th, 1966. Most of those present at the auction imagined that a sporting millionaire might well be keen to buy, many feared that perhaps some tycoon with plans for marinas and holiday camps would be waiting to move in. Only a few realised that Norfolk County Council's Education Committee were interested. Dr Harold Hudson, the committee's chairman, and Dr F. Lincoln Ralphs, chief education officer, had seen the potential of the property, and it was their bid of £37,000 which was successful.

How Hill House as it appeared on the cover of the sale catalogue, 1966.

The *Eastern Evening News* carried the story the same day, and told its readers that the County's spokesman had refused to say why the Council had bought the property. "You will find out in due course", he said. In fact the County spent an undisclosed sum on renovating and remodelling the interior, and renewing the thatch, and then opened How Hill as the County Residential Education Centre. It was intended to accommodate children and teachers on field study courses, conferences and training events.

The official opening of How Hill in its new form was performed by E. A. ('Ted') Ellis, the Norfolk naturalist and "personality", on Saturday September 7th 1968, although in fact the first warden, E. B. Loy, had been offering courses there since the spring of that year. Ted Ellis planted a tree at How Hill that day, a *Sequoiadendron giganteum*, less than three feet high, now a towering feature of the Fisherman's Field. He said that the centre could give the children of Norfolk "a share in a paradise".

The Drawing Room of How Hill House from the sale catalogue:
now the Lincoln Ralphs Room.

The Sun Parlour of How Hill House from the sale catalogue:
now Lady Mayhew's Room.

An aerial view of How Hill House taken as the centre was being prepared
for its first group of Norfolk schoolchildren in 1967.

The new centre offered residential facilities, a camping field, and
a nature trail. Thus the pattern of activity at this unique field centre
was established. Children had to pay for their visits, but the centre
received a substantial allocation from the Education Committee's
annual budget.

Sir Lincoln Ralphs, Chief Education Officer for Norfolk, 1950 to 1974.

There were, surprisingly, some difficulties with the community at large. Even before the official opening there were fears that the right of anglers to fish the river would be lost. Before the sale, permits could be bought from the Boardman family for two shillings, but local angling clubs received letters from the new owners telling them "in future no fishing will be allowed on the estate". However this problem was resolved and fishing permits were sold by the Council. Later, a dispute arose about public use of the staithe and the footpath to it. People were told not to use the path when courses were in progress, and "No Mooring" signs appeared on the staithe. Ludham Parish Council was incensed, and took their protest to the Labour MP for North Norfolk, Mr Bert Hazell. It took two years of persistent campaigning by the parish before the Council eventually commissioned a local public enquiry. Since the path was formerly used for carriage of goods between the staithe and the windmill, there was a strong case. The mention of the track in the Ludham Enclosure Order of 1802 was apparently irrefutable evidence of its status as a public right of way, and the enquiry inspector reported in favour of the parish. Eventually his report was accepted by the County Council, and the staithe is now regarded as a parish staithe with a public right of way leading to it. The campaign left a legacy of suspicion however, and the adverse publicity was most unwelcome.

Turf Fen Drainage Windmill as it appeared in the 1970s.

The centre settled into its routine, and children began to enjoy the delights of the estate. Many had their imagination fired by glimpses of swallowtail butterflies and emperor moths. Lincoln Ralphs took a personal interest in the centre, and encouraged the head keeper, Bob Smithson, to share his extensive knowledge of man and nature in Broadland with the children. A central feature of all environmental courses became an experience of the way of life of the marshman, with the old marsh tools, the reed harvest, and the traditions of the Broads – all explained by the marshman himself.

The chief education officer, by now Sir Lincoln Ralphs, brought the Secretary of State for Education and Science to How Hill in January 1974. Whether this visit was influential in forming the Minister's view of the Broads, we may never know, but the right honourable lady's government, twelve years later, added the Broads Bill to their programme of legislation. Mrs Thatcher's visit to How Hill, when she met representatives of local teaching organisations, was part of a two day tour of Norfolk schools and colleges, and she described How Hill as "a wonderful institution".

Bob Smithson cutting How Hill reed in the County Council days.

Bob Smithson, in his last year at How Hill, quants a small group of children across the river in the reed lighter, and talks to them about the reed harvest. At the time these photographs were taken, the decision to close How Hill as a County Council centre had already been announced.

A postcard view of How Hill during the County Council era.

Shortly afterwards, Sir Lincoln Ralphs retired, on the occasion of reorganisation of local government. A retirement dinner was held for him at How Hill, and those present realised that How Hill was losing its most formidable ally and supporter. From then on, How Hill would be just one of several costly county centres, no longer under the personal favour of a nationally respected chief officer.

In 1982, a subcommittee of the County Education Committee presented a report on the residential centres in Norfolk, and recommended that How Hill should be closed and sold. It was a tempting target, hugely expensive to run and including not only a highly desirable and saleable mansion, and two smaller houses, but also a 350 acre estate which fitted very badly in the property portfolio of an education department. Rumours of the closure began to spread, and a campaign to change the Council's mind began. Looking back at the early stages of the campaign, there was no clear lead, and no co-ordination of effort. Several letters appeared in the local press, backed up by one or two leading articles. A certain amount of television coverage was achieved. Ted Ellis gave his full support to the campaign, and the North Norfolk MP, Ralph Howell, tried to influence the ruling Conservative group of the County Council.

However, the campaign was very confused. The Broads Authority were criticised for trying to buy the property when in fact they were trying, behind the scenes, to secure the future of the nature reserve and to find some way of keeping the educational facility going. However, it is true to say that they gave close consideration to a plan to relocate their offices at How Hill, and house the educational activities in a timber building outside. The councillors who were keenest to close the centre made some conflicting statements which enraged those who worked at the centre and upset local campaigners. The full story of the closure will never be told, but many factors which were only discussed behind closed doors had an influence. In the event, the Council would not change their policy on closure. They sold the estate to the Broads Authority for £125,000, and they were negotiating with a private company who wanted to turn the house into a convalescent home. At the last minute the Council agreed to hold the negotiations on the sale of the house for a fortnight, enabling a hastily convened steering group to step in and find some way of acquiring the house.

It was a campaign of many individuals, but two in particular worked hard to find a purchaser for the house who would let How Hill continue as an educational centre. Keith McDougall and Bryan Read tried to interest the Carnegie UK Trust and the National Trust in the project – and interestingly the National Trust showed some enthusiasm. The regional committee decided on balance that the educational role of How Hill, and the need to admit casual visitors, were not compatible and reluctantly decided not to become involved. However the main breakthrough came as a result of an approach to Peter Sharman, chief general manager of the Norwich Union Insurance Group. The world famous company agreed to buy the house – for about £120,000 – and lease it back to a charitable trust which would run the centre.

The immense relief at this unique deal did not disguise the major problems which lay ahead. The warden of How Hill, Mr P. D. Lee, was redeployed as the County's environmental studies advisory teacher, but the other employees at the centre were made redundant. Two of them were taken on by the Broads Authority to work on their new estate. The Authority was expected to lease the whole estate to the new Trust, but in the event they only granted a lease on a small area (the water garden, camp site, Fisherman's field and neighbouring ground, some small woodlands and Toad Hole Cottage – 27 acres in all). The two houses which had been occupied by the warden and the head keeper were sold off separately by the County Council, netting a further £90,000 for the County Treasurer, but leaving no accommodation for residential staff.

The complex legal arrangements to create the new Trust were the task of a steering committee under the chairmanship of solicitor Nigel Hill. There were innumerable problems but the Charity Commissioners and Inland Revenue were eventually satisfied. A problem arose with the leases, because although the Norwich Union had granted a 99 year lease on the house, the Broads Authority, having made a similar offer, were told by the Department of the Environment that this was not permitted. In the event, the Authority granted a seven year, renewable lease. Neither landlord gave the new Trust any money, nor indeed any promises, but eventually, on April 1st 1984, the How Hill Trust came into being, with scarcely any resources other than an overdraft facility negotiated at commercial rates with Barclays Bank.

How Hill House: The Study Centre for the Broads.

5 How Hill in Trust

The establishment of the How Hill Trust brought the Norwich Union Insurance Group and the Broads Authority into unique partnership. It was very quickly clear however that uniqueness was no guarantee of survival, and that the arrangement was very far removed from sponsorship. It also emerged that the new Trust would have to be run as a business, with VAT and Inland Revenue registration, with approval from a wide range of official bodies, and with a fully commercial approach to its staff and its customers. Additionally its educational role, enshrined in its Trust Deed, needed to be conducted in a professional manner, with teaching methods and objectives fully thought out to conform to syllabus requirements and the high standards offered in the very best field centres. How all this could be achieved, particularly when the centre was starved of resources, was a major nightmare – but the general consensus is that the Trust has met every possible target. The early critics – and there were very many – have almost entirely been confounded.

How Hill House in June.

The keys to this success have been threefold – activity, promotion of the centre, and sheer hard work. It will only be appropriate to consider the first of these. One of the problems which was identified during the rescue campaign was that How Hill had been closed for periods during school holidays, weekends, and much of the winter. The Trust could not afford to leave the house empty for so long, so it set about the task of finding users for as much of the year as possible. Holidays and courses for the general public were a major innovation. Training courses for youngsters starting in employment, weekends for colleges, polytechnics and universities, conferences for magistrates, social workers, probation officers, health authority managers, youth leaders, and head teachers were all added to the programme. A hectic series of summer buffets were provided for the Broads Society, the Norfolk Society, the Gilbert and Sullivan Society, and a variety of special interest groups. How Hill hosted a summer ball and a wedding reception. A new book was launched; art exhibitions and antique fairs were held, and Ted Ellis gave a splendid illustrated soiree entitled 'A Tapestry of Nature', sadly one of his last public events.

Steamboat Rally, How Hill Staithe.

Public opening is not normally compatible with residential activity, but nonetheless the Trust was able to promote more Open Days than ever before, together with a Steam Boat Rally, annual Butterfly Festivals, (in conjunction with the Norfolk Branch of the British Butterfly Conservation Society), mystery nature trails and activity days, and a major conservation festival as part of European Year of the Environment (EYE on the Broads, 1987). An exceptional and quite unexpected winter event occurred when teaching assistant, Martin McDonnell, spotted a transatlantic vagrant Black and White Warbler in the grounds, and the paths were opened to thousands of bird watchers, including some from Belgium and the Netherlands.

Ted Ellis prepares to answer questions from the public at "EYE on the Broads".

The net result of all this hectic activity was to prove that How Hill could be a viable enterprise without the support of Norfolk's ratepayers, and yet still provide a first class educational facility for the county's children. It was evident from the beginning however that the centre needed a major programme of renovation. With this in mind, a public

Appeal was launched in March 1985 under the patronage of the Lord Lieutenant of Norfolk, Sir Timothy Colman, who had been a frequent guest of the Boardman family in earlier times. There were some considerable disappointments with the Appeal, particularly the poor response from the general public and from those who had been so vocal during the closure campaign. Nonetheless, some very substantial gifts were received from local charities such as the Town Close Estate Charity, the Alderman Norman's Foundation and the John Jarrold Trust. National donors included the Wates Foundation, the Ernest Cook Trust, the Lankelly, Hayward and Wolfson Foundations. Commercial companies offered more limited support but the Trust was particularly indebted to Philips Petroleum and to Arco British; international recognition came in the form of a major grant from the Amoco Foundation of Chicago. Some prominent local concerns made covenanted donations, notably Blakes, Hoseasons, Eastern Counties Newspapers and Anglia Television. Eventually enough was collected to make a start on the refurbishment of the residential accommodation at How Hill, which took place during the first three months of 1987.

The view from How Hill.

The Trust had official visits from many celebrated guests, notably Lord Belstead, the Sports Minister Colin Moynihan, Brian Redhead, the Chairmen of Anglia Television, of the Nature Conservancy Council, and of Anglian Water. The select committee of MP's investigating the 'Broads Bill' visited the centre, and were particularly impressed with the thatching frame where children gain first-hand experience of working with reeds, 'leggatts' and 'brotches' – "that's where we train Thatchers" they were told, to much partisan amusement. Even before their visit, Sir John Wells, MP for Maidstone, had praised the How Hill Trust in the parliamentary debate on the Broads Bill: "… I commend to hon. members in all parts of the House the How Hill Trust, which is perhaps one of the most imaginative attempts at bringing the charms of the Broadland area to the nation as a whole …" (Hansard, 1-12-86). Television and press coverage of the centre's progress was handsome, including two extended presentations of the Trust's work and several shorter reports.

The Boardman family at the dedication of the Boardman Room:
left to right, Christopher Boardman, David Holmes, Mrs Joan Lynde,
Humphrey Boardman and Michael Boardman.

Meanwhile the Broads Authority was busy with the estate. Restoration of the dyke system and clearance of the invading scrub were major priorities. There are now several miles of improved dyke, much of it with impressive growth of water plants, and the annual reed harvest has been dramatically improved. A new thatched boathouse replaced the old corrugated shed, a nature trail was opened, and Toad Hole Cottage was restored and opened as a marshland museum. The most innovative improvement was the establishment of a wildlife water trail, using a quiet, pollution-free electric boat, taking small groups of visitors into otherwise unseen parts of the estate.

The Norfolk Windmills Trust was also active at How Hill. Using the services of the expert millwright, John Lawn, the Trust replaced the cap, fantail, and sails of Turf Fen drainage windmill. The skills and energy of John in this complex technical work transformed the mill, and in due course it was hoped to have the mechanism fully operational and pumping. Norfolk's other celebrated millwright, Richard Seago, restored a unique hollow post windpump which was rediscovered at Ranworth, and the Trust relocated this structure at How Hill. Considerable quantities of concrete, sand, and engineering bricks were delivered to the new site in the winter of 1987-88, and in due course this remarkable little windpump was to have been used to control the water levels on the grazing land, known as the Clayrack marshes. Subsequently, lack of funds for repairs and other problems have seen both these drainage mills decline again.

The climate cannot be said to have helped any of the agencies involved with How Hill. Seventy five years to the day after the 1912 floods, the marshland was again flooded in August 1987, and water levels remained generally high for six months. The centre was twice cut off by snowstorms, in January 1985 (when Sheringham Primary School were in residence) and for more than a week in January 1987 (when building work was delayed). Above all, there was spectacular and irreparable damage when the unnamed hurricane struck on the night of October 15-16, 1987. More than 250 trees were lost on the estate, with one or two very sad casualties, such as the bitternut hickory in the front garden, planted as a seed before the First World War by E. T. Boardman.

The Boardman family have supported the new venture from the beginning and the Trust was delighted to hold a special day for the family, in June 1987, to say thank you for their strong backing and continued interest during difficult times. Christopher Boardman unveiled a new sign beneath "Hitler's Oak", recalling his Olympic triumph, and dedicated the old, well-loved pine-panelled drawing room as 'The Boardman Room'. How Hill lost a friend and supporter when he died in September of the same year.

**Unveiling the new plaque at the foot of "Hitler's Oak", June 1987.
Front row, left to right: David Holmes, Stephen Boardman,
Mrs Joan Lynde, Christopher Boardman and Sue Holmes.**

The Trust was also able to commemorate Sir Lincoln Ralphs, who was Chief Education Officer for Norfolk when How Hill came on the market in 1966, and whose inspiration it was to buy and convert How Hill into an educational centre. Lady Ralphs opened the 'Lincoln Ralphs Room' at How Hill in April 1987, which had been remodelled thanks to a generous grant from the memorial funds to Sir Lincoln.

Lady Enid Ralphs straightens the photograph of her late husband, the visionary Chief Education Officer behind How Hill's educational success, as she dedicated the Lincoln Ralphs Room to his memory.

Progress was such that, by the summer of 1988, the Trustees were able to take stock and think of the future. All seemed set fair, and the Trust was surely an established feature of Broadland life, with strong landlords standing in the wings, with a tremendous groundswell of interest, and with an enviable and growing reputation in its particular field of environmental education. But security can never be guaranteed, in a body without appropriate funding, and with the chequered history of How Hill, nothing was taken for granted. The Trustees were happy with early progress and took great comfort from the support of the Boardman family, but had no intention of becoming either complacent or self-satisfied, and there was still much to do. Broadland was recovering, slowly but surely, and the Trust stood ready to play its small part in the long and steady process of regeneration. The rescue of How Hill was intended to ensure that the next generation should still care about the countryside in general, and the Broads in particular, and to foster a welcome but significant trend towards environmental revitalisation.

6 Securing the Future

The two decades which bring the How Hill Story up to date, those years to 2011, were characterised by frenetic, often feverish activity. Determined never to miss a chance to make use of the Centre, and never to miss an opportunity to gain some income for the Trust, I demanded total commitment from the hard-pressed How Hill staff. The level of activity, and the nature of the stress generated, can be gleamed from a comment made by a senior Norfolk County Council Officer one memorable morning. Arriving to open a two-day conference of County Careers Officers and teachers due to start at 10 a.m., he encountered the previous evening's residents departing after breakfast. "Knowing How Hill so well, I'm surprised you didn't sub-let the Centre between 9 and 10 a.m." was his sardonic remark.

June 20th 1988 was a high-profile day. The County Council had successfully steered the *Norfolk & Suffolk Broads Act* on to the statute book, and decided that How Hill was the ideal place to hold a 'Broads Celebration' to mark the event. The Department of the Environment Parliamentary Under Secretary, Hon. Colin Moynihan MP., undertook the keynote speech, and around 200 guests from national and local organisations were present for a series of presentations and speeches, and, of course, a lavish buffet lunch.

Ever since the early days of crisis when the Centre had been under such pressing threat of closure, the idea of a 'Friends of How Hill' had been under discussion. However, the idea needed to be translated into reality by means of a constitution, a committee, and promotional literature and a group of enthusiasts had to be recruited to bring the organisation into being. Eventually, on Thursday 27th October 1988 an inaugural meeting was held, in the Assembly House in Norwich, and the 'Friends of How Hill' was formally initiated, and Basil de Iongh, at that time Projects Officer with the Broads Authority, was elected Chairman. A few years later, as a result of changes in legislation, it became necessary to re-write the constitution and re-launch the 'Friends' as a registered charity in its own right. Over the years the group has raised many thousands of pounds for How Hill, and its long-time Secretary, Sue Holmes, has arranged dozens of special events for members.

Visits of senior politicians and public figures are always shrouded in secrecy during the months of planning which lead up to them.

The Prince of Wales visits How Hill, November 1988.

The Director forgets to bow to H R H Prince Charles
at the front door of How Hill House.

However, it is not particularly difficult to spot that something is afoot. Serious, sober, suited gentlemen appear at odd times in huddles in fields, tracks, and marshes, deep in earnest conversation, and frequently consulting clipboards. Prince Charles' visit to How Hill, on 29th November 1988, was a happy and relaxed day, despite the preliminary processes which had dominated the preceding weeks. His Royal Highness arrived by helicopter of the Queen's Flight, which was beautifully polished and gleaming red, and the Prince took his place in the Boardman Room for the standard slide show on the problems of the Broads. He visited the marshes, and then came back to meet the assembled dignitaries of Norfolk in the Lincoln Ralphs Room. Eventually he was released from the formality of the visit for a chance to sail on the Wherry Hathor, even taking the helm on the way up to Barton Broad.

Prime Minister and Marshman: both at ease in front of a camera.

The security put in place for the visit of Rt. Hon. Mrs Margaret Thatcher, Prime Minister, on Wednesday 23rd May 1990 was unparalleled in How Hill's history. A spare helicopter in case of air attack, snipers in the marsh and atop the windmill, sniffer dogs on patrol throughout the previous night, the road and river both sealed off by the police, a dedicated "safe" room and guns by the dozen: all were part of this exceptional event. It was made all the more challenging for How Hill as it was planned for a normal school day: 54 girls from the Junior Department of Norwich High School were in residence, and although they did not know it until the evening before, Mrs Thatcher was intending to meet them.

The day dawned bright and warm, and the official convoy, headed by a dozen or more police motorcycles, duly arrived, followed soon after by the two RAF helicopters, one of which disgorged the Prime Minister and her team, and the other hovered ominously until it was declared that How Hill was secure. At the front door Mrs Thatcher chatted knowledgeably about our reed thatch, and I remarked with a smile that we would expect her to know all about that sort of thing. From then until the end of the visit, she hardly left my side and seemed completely at ease. In the gardens for example she said that she loved gardens, but was almost never allowed to visit them because her security people objected. Towards the end of the visit her senior aide nudged me, and told me to tell her that she was over an hour behind schedule, and that it was time to move on. "They always say that" was her terse response and she carried on with chatting to other guests.

Prime Minister Margaret Thatcher gets a briefing on the problems of the Broads from Rebecca Lindner, How Hill May 1990.

For How Hill the undoubted highlight of the morning was when Mrs Thatcher pulled up a chair at a table of eight young girls and asked them what they were doing at the Centre. Rebecca Lindner, not yet 12 years old, stood up and delivered, word-perfect, a lecture on the Eutrophication of the Broads. I was astonished; we had not planned anything of the kind, Rebecca did it entirely of her own volition, and it was a *tour de force*. For the next month or so, every time the national television news needed footage of Margaret Thatcher's interest in education or science or both, the same sequence of Mrs Thatcher and Rebecca Lindner was played, to my great delight.

Despite such excitement, and the great publicity generated thereby, the central issue of how to fund How Hill remained a constant concern. One of the supporters of the project from the beginning was Mr Freddie Self, formerly Deputy Head at the Norwich School. On one of his regular visits to How Hill I managed to focus his thoughts on the possibility of establishing an endowment fund for How Hill. Mr Self was Chairman of the Norwich Town Close Estate Charity, an education and welfare charity which has particular interests in the City of Norwich, but he undertook to put our case to his board. With his support, we eventually secured the huge sum of £50,000 to initiate the new fund, which was to be known as the Boardman Fund. Interest from the Fund would be used to support children coming to How Hill from poorer backgrounds, as well as to make a contribution towards the huge and growing burden of repairs and maintenance for the house. An appeal was launched to encourage more contributions to the Fund, and today its capital value is more than £100,000 and the income continues to assist the Trust's endeavours.

The Freshwater Ecology Centre: the How Hill Trust's Millennium Project.

In the run up to the Millennium, the whole nation was minded to complete some key projects to mark this astonishing milestone. At How Hill our efforts were geared towards replacement of our only scientific facility, an elderly "mobile" classroom. Anything but mobile, it was too cold in the winter (so cold that the water had to be turned off at the mains for three months each winter to prevent burst pipes) and too hot in the summer. Cramped and creaking, it was quite unsuitable for its intended use as a laboratory. Plans were drawn up for a new building, but progress was slow and planning issues appeared insuperable. At the same time, the Broads Authority's bid for their Millennium Project, 'Clearwater 2000', the restoration of Barton Broad, was rejected because of the lack of educational and public benefit criteria. The Authority's Interpretation Officer, Diana Shipp, called me to see if we could pool resources to put this application jointly back on track. In the end, a revised version of 'Clearwater 2000' proved to be a winner, with huge benefits for water space in Barton Broad and beyond, and our own 'Freshwater Ecology Centre' took shape, thanks to funding from the Millennium Commission and the Broads Authority. The new building included a laboratory as well as a spacious studio style meeting room, which has been used to further enhance the range of activities offered at How Hill. The new building won "green" awards from both the Norfolk Society and North Norfolk District Council.

**The Pleasure Wherry *Hathor* celebrates her Centenary
at How Hill, August 2005.**

One of the most significant milestones in How Hill's history slipped by without notice or comment. Norfolk County Council had owned and managed the centre for 17 years, and at some point during 2001 the How Hill Trust overtook this figure, quietly becoming the senior partner in the history of provision of environmental education on this site.

The south front of How Hill House shimmers in summer sunshine.

During the last few years of the twentieth Century, and into the new millennium, difficulties began to emerge with the owners of the house. Norwich Union Insurance Group ceased to be a mutual company, and was floated on the stock market, and then merged with several other large companies. As CGNU, they became less interested in Norfolk projects in general and How Hill in particular. Goodwill remained, but practical assistance became very difficult to secure. The ownership of the House was no longer seen as a gesture of support for a community project, but as a liability: a building which needed a good deal of maintenance and yet which produced only a modest rental income. Acrimonious debate resulted in an uneasy stalemate, but eventually Trust Chairman Jonathan Peel CBE managed to convince the company that the freehold should be given to the Trust. In April 2002, after a mountain of legal paperwork had been sifted, the freehold of the house and gardens were handed over to the Trustees, and Norwich Union, by now called Aviva plc., ceased to have anything further to do with How Hill. The company even refused to insure the property, giving a very challenging start to the new arrangements, and delaying the hand-over for 15 days.

February frost.

This change represented a huge new opportunity for the Trustees, although the costs of ownership were seen as potentially very damaging. Inevitably more money would be required in future, but to be spent on a building which could no longer be taken away from us. The obvious response was to share this wonderful, yet sobering news with the public and seek further support. Thus, on 25th October 2003, the Lord Lieutenant of Norfolk, Sir Timothy Colman K.G., launched the How Hill Centenary Appeal, seeking to raise £250,000. The appeal was a great success, partly as a result of two substantial legacies from supporters. Before 2003 the largest legacy received by the Trust was from Beryl, Lady Mayhew, who had known the Boardman family in her younger days, and who celebrated her 100th birthday at How Hill in 1997. Two ladies who died in 2003 left handsome legacies which changed

How Hill's fortunes forever. We shall always remember Mrs. Hetty Myers (8th May 1909 to 24th February 2003), who was well known in Norwich as her late husband had been Minister at the Princes Street Congregational Church, and Mrs Audrey Wilson (29th September 1923 to 16th June 2003) who was a strong supporter of How Hill and a regular participant on courses at the centre. Legacies are a vital part of the finances of the Trust, and further gifts have come in this way from Miss Pamela Oakes, well known as Secretary to many local organisations, including the Broads Society and the Norfolk Wherry Trust, and from Mrs Marjorie Whitby, a former supporter and regular course member.

The Centenary Year of How Hill was slightly difficult to pin down, as building started in 1903 and the house was not occupied until 1905, but the date over the front door is 1904, so 2004 was clearly the right year to celebrate not only 100 years of How Hill, but 20 years of the How Hill Trust. A Centenary Garden Party was held on Saturday 3rd July, and a Celebration of How Hill on Saturday 25th September. Both days were well attended and greatly enjoyed, and inevitably both were accompanied by windy, wet conditions. A further Centenary was celebrated the following year, that of the Pleasure Wherry *Hathor*, 100 years old and still sailing. Edward Thomas Boardman had designed the interior of this venerable vessel, and his daughter Joan had released white doves at both the original launching and her 1989 re-launch after extensive restoration work. The *Hathor* was for many years based during the summer at How Hill, and the Boardman and Colman families jointly enjoyed many happy Broadland cruises on board. The Centenary sailing on 2nd August 2005, followed by a lavish party at How Hill, was a chance to cement the relationship between the How Hill Trust and the newly established Wherry Yacht Charter Charitable Trust, set up to preserve the *Hathor* and her sister Wherry Yachts *Olive* and *Norada*.

Three members of the Boardman family who had provided such encouragement and support for the developing How Hill Trust sadly never saw the Centenary events. Edward Thomas Boardman's daughter Joan Caroline (Mrs Lynde) died on 17th March 1998, and her brothers Humphrey Colman Boardman and Michael Russell Boardman died on 15th June 1998 and 5th September 2002 respectively. There were also changes on the Board of Trustees, and the first Chairman of Trustees, Keith McDougall, stood down and was succeeded by Rev. Jonathan Peel, MC, CBE, DL, DCL, and in turn the Chairmanship was taken over by Nick Price FRICS. Meanwhile, Broads Authority Marshman Eric Edwards, forever associated with How Hill thanks to frequent television appearances and press photo essays, went to Buckingham Palace to receive the well-deserved and unexpected honour of an M.B.E. (14th October 2004).

School day visits and miscellaneous non-residential activities had begun to be a major part of the How Hill calendar in the late 1980s, and wet weather often caused these visits to be disappointing. A second-hand marquee which blew over in an autumn gale provided temporary accommodation, but it was clear that something more permanent would be required. At the same time the interest in reed-cutting, sedge and thatching was a stimulus to developing further activities and courses at How Hill, against a background of catastrophic decline in these traditional Broadland activities. The Trust was keen to promote understanding of the issues involved by means of the 'Living Marshes Project' and campaigned for the funds to take this forward. After much frustration and intense planning difficulties, a traditional oak framed and thatched building was erected on the north field at How Hill, and was named in honour of Colin O'Riordan, whose brother Tim had been a Trustee and a donor. This splendid new project was formally opened by Norman Lamb MP on 26th September 2006, and later received an Environmental Award from CPRE Norfolk.

Norman Lamb MP opens the Colin O'Riordan Building for the How Hill Trust's Living Marshes Project, September 2006.

The Colin O'Riordan Building.

During recent years there have been many changes in the Broads Authority, a partner in the How Hill project from its inception. We continue to lease land from the Authority including the water gardens and the two fields, and we were delighted when a process of review re-established this lease, and secured an annual Service Level Agreement Payment which makes a real contribution to the ever-increasing costs of this enterprise. The Authority's How Hill Nature Reserve was officially designated as a National Nature Reserve on 15th May 2006, and this new status can only enhance How Hill's position as one of the country's most cherished environmental study centres.

Although circumstances contrived to prevent proper celebration of the Trust's Silver Jubilee Year in 2009, we did at least have a Garden Party to mark the occasion, and a short commemorative booklet was produced for sale to visitors. Simon Partridge, once a teaching assistant at How Hill, but by now a Trustee, used How Hill as the venue for the Civic Reception, which inaugurated his year as Chairman of North Norfolk District Council. The undoubted highlight of the evening was the first public performance, by the beautiful and engaging Royal Harpist Claire Jones, of "How Hill", a composition by Patrick Hawes, formerly Classic FM's *Composer in Residence*. The lyrical melody of this evocative piece was enhanced movingly by the natural sounds of a summer evening at How Hill, drifting into the marquee from the woods and marshes.

Silver Jubilee Celebrations at How Hill, 26 July 2009.

Centre Manager Sue Holmes at the front door.

2009 also marked 25 years of service with the How Hill Trust by both Ruby Edwards and Sue Holmes, but 2010 brought the end of this era with the retirement of both of them, in particular Sue from her post of Centre Manager. In the event it was proved that no one individual could fill her shoes, not least because of her long term commitment to the Friends of How Hill as their "Honorary" Secretary. My own involvement with How Hill dates back to my sixth form years: I joined a natural history course in 1968, to be followed later by regular visits as a lecturer and teacher in the 1970s and 80s, and by appointment in October 1983 as the Trust's founding Director. Now retirement beckons. More change will follow in due course, and the future will undoubtedly present its own challenges, but the Trust is here to stay, and we have secured a place in the hearts and minds of all those who love the Broads and the wider Norfolk countryside.

Girls from Blofield Primary School admire the view from Room 6, their home for the next few days.

7 How Hill as Architecture

Edward Thomas Boardman, architect and owner of How Hill, was not an architect who would have wished to identify with any particular movement or school of thought. His work shows that he could use a variety of styles, tailoring his designs to the needs of the client, and to the purpose and function of the building. However, it is clear that when he came to design his own holiday home, and later to enlarge it into his main residence, he was seeking to build a significant house combining the latest ideas of comfort and convenience with the best of the past. There were therefore many influences on his plans.

Two views of "The White House" at How Hill nearing completion, 1904-05.

Dr Bill Wilson, revising the Norfolk volumes of Pevsner's '*Buildings of England*', describes the style of How Hill as 'Jacobean Vernacular'. 'Jacobean' is appropriate because the timber-mullioned windows, complete with leaded panes, as well as other details of the house, would not look out of place on a much older building. Blickling Hall is only twenty miles away, and is described as 'one of the major Jacobean houses in England': it dates from 1618. 'Vernacular' suggests that the house owes much to the cottage style of village houses in the district, few if any of which were actually designed by architects. They are houses which appear to have grown organically from the soil, using materials made from whatever was to hand locally.

It is not possible that Edward Boardman could have been unmoved by the prevailing views of artists and architects of his time. He may have had a healthy disregard for some of their more fanciful ideas, but he had excellent contacts within his profession and would have been conversant with the tide of ideas. The dominant theme in English architecture at the end of the Victorian era and into Edwardian times was the 'Arts and Crafts' Movement. The Arts and Crafts Movement is associated with such eminent Victorians as John Ruskin, William Morris and Gertrude Jekyll. The movement espoused four principles, which extended far beyond architecture and into all forms of creative arts, even for some of its advocates into the realms of political philosophy. The principles were

- ◆ Unity of Design
- ◆ Joy in Labour
- ◆ Individualism
- ◆ Regionalism

The results of combining these four principles is that architects of the period made sure that their buildings related to the landscape in which they were sited, and selected their materials with the greatest care, using those available in the immediate locality wherever possible. They turned their backs on the products of industrial Britain, preferring to use traditional skills and established craftsmen. They hated the mass-produced uniformity which had been such a feature of the Victorian success story, and they delighted in individuality and originality. Their new houses "were considered successful if, while not imitative of one particular style, they gave the impression of having evolved naturally through the centuries." (Elizabeth Cumming, *The Arts and Crafts Movement*, London, 1991)

A Jacobean Entrance Front?

What has been written above in a general sense as descriptive of Arts and Crafts buildings is particularly apt when applied to How Hill. The site is superbly chosen; the house relates perfectly to its unique setting overlooking the marshes. The expanse of thatch harvested from its own reed and sedge beds makes a satisfying statement of unity with its location. The house was brick built, but none of the bricks can be seen as the surface is rendered with roughcast. This might be seen as strange, but the actual site of the house had been a sand and gravel pit for some years: what stronger link with the ground could be devised than using this very material to complete the house?

Edward Boardman designed all the window catches, stays, casements, door handles, latches and hinges, thus maintaining the unity of design. He then employed craftsmen to make up all these items: nothing mass produced was permitted. He hinted at traditional East Anglian craft skills by using decorations on the chimneys and pargetting on the window surrounds. Bay window, parapet, door hood and stone steps all add to the slightly antiquarian impression the front of the house provides. Many visitors are convinced the house is much older until they notice the date (1904) over the front door. There are other details which are very much in line with the concepts embraced by the Arts and Crafts movement. The orientation of the house makes sure that all the main rooms enjoy a southerly aspect: all the working rooms (bathrooms and kitchens) are on the utilitarian north side. All the main rooms on each of the three floors are approached by a corridor running the full length of the house. The external chimney on the eastern wall of the main reception room appears to grow organically from the ground, and is suitably imposing (it was originally much taller). Vehicles, a product of the factory age, were not permitted to approach the front of the house, and are to this day excluded by an archway and double right angled entry route.

One of Edward Boardman's great passions was gardening, and it is clear that he designed the house and garden to be a single concept. The most striking feature of the How Hill gardens is the maze-like pattern created by the yew hedges. This divides the garden into separate spaces; in short the garden has 'rooms' just like the house. The link between the house and garden is emphasized by the loggia, built into the hillside beneath the main room of the house. A semi circle, open at the front, with pillars and open sides, provides a space which is either garden or house, depending on the weather or on one's perspective.

The lasting contribution of architects of the Arts and Crafts Movement was to open their houses to sunlight, dispelling the stifling Victorian gloom of earlier times. How Hill was originally planned as a holiday home, so sunlight was even more welcome, and the huge curved windows which were added in 1916 did so much to enhance this aspect of the property. The room now known as Lady Mayhew's Room was, to the Boardman family, the Sun Parlour, and early photographs show them enjoying the southerly aspect even on winter days. Bill Wilson puts it neatly:

> "...the emphasis on large windows as sun-traps overlooking the Broads is a fairly emphatic indication of the Edwardians' attitude to nature as a somewhat less dangerous thing than it was considered thirty years before."

The main reception room of How Hill House:
"large windows as sun-traps overlooking the Broads..."

8 The How Hill Water Gardens

Technically a bog garden, this part of How Hill has come to be known as the Water Gardens and is most famous for its array of sub-tropical colours during the azalea season. It was planned by the original owner and designer of How Hill, Edward Thomas Boardman, and was for many years his abiding passion.

The area was once a piece of rough grazing marsh, with one or two ancient willows. The transformation was effected by digging out the peat to make shallow pools and using it to build beds about 18 inches above the water level. In this way the lime hating plants which thrive in peat soils can be given favoured conditions. Once open on all sides, trees have grown up around the garden giving it a sheltered aspect, and it always presents a haven of calm within the grounds.

The How Hill Water Gardens at their best – the third week of May.

One of the most notable changes since Mr Boardman's time is the loss of bamboos. There are still one or two small clumps, but most of the bigger stands have died out. It seems that bamboo flowers only after a very long time – many years – and only when conditions are just right. The plant then dies, sure in the knowledge that seed has been set for the next generation. Unfortunately the British summer is not hot enough to encourage germination of the seeds, and the bamboo disappears.

Azaleas, Royal Fern, Gunnera – and Water Soldier – are all characteristic How Hill Water Garden plants.

However the azaleas and rhododendrons continue to flourish. They tolerate shade as long as there is a patch of clear sky immediately above them, and as some plants die each winter gaps can be filled with young plants which have seeded in the garden. They like the acid peat soil and require constant moisture at their roots – a problem in recent summers when drought conditions have prevailed. Their colours and scents combine to transport visitors on exotic flights of fancy, but sadly their flowering season is over in less than a month.

Many of the unusual plants introduced by Mr Boardman and his sons have disappeared, most notably the blue Himalayan poppies and many types of lily. As the Trust develops, we hope to reinstate some of these lost plants, and hope that the gardens will again colour throughout the seasons. Some of the lilies persist, and the most exceptional is the giant wood lily, sometimes six to eight feet high, impressive in early autumn but in flower for only a few days.

Meconopsis, the Himalayan Blue Poppy, was re-established in the Water Gardens in 2011, after an absence of 40 years.

The water in the pools is often crystal clear, reminding visitors of the days when the Broads themselves were "gin-clear". Some of the pools are spring-fed, as they are so low-lying, and most of them have secret colonies of fish and small water creatures. The Boardman family used to set bow nets for tench and other fish in the ponds, and often took remarkable catches. Now the fish are smaller and fewer, but a ripple sometimes pinpoints the presence of a pike or carp. Flourishing in some of these pools are species of plants and small invertebrates (or 'minibeasts') which were once common but are now almost entirely absent from the Broads. To most visitors, the combination of brightly coloured far-eastern flowers with delicate and unusual native plants is entrancing and adds much to the character of the gardens.

The How Hil Azaleas are a feast for the eye in late Spring.

In essence, the How Hill water gardens represent a 'natural' garden. Many species of English wild plants are found in the gardens, and we may never discover which are native and which were established by planting. In the heart of the garden are several ancient clumps of royal fern, a majestic plant of marshlands, now rare in the wild. Growing on an island nearby are drifts of bog pimpernel, showing delicate pink flowers in June. Around one pond can be found the tiny yellow florets of marsh St John's wort, now very scarce in the marshes of Broadland. The ponds are often fringed with ubiquitous Norfolk reed, and some have impressive spikes of greater reedmace, usually wrongly identified as bulrush.

The water plants themselves are more certainly native, with the striking exception of the pink waterlilies. Sometimes the water plants grow in such profusion that the dykes become choked and need to be cleaned out using the traditional long-handled tools – crome and meag – of the Norfolk marshes. Several water plants produce flowers above the surface, including the water soldier, water violet and bogbean. The water soldier has sharp, upright, spear-shaped leaves protecting a trio of white petals, whereas the bogbean has feathery white and pink flowers.

Autumn colours can also be spectacular in the How Hill Water Gardens.

Royal Fern, *Osmunda regalis*, a native of the Broads district, is at its best on an October morning in the Water Gardens.

The garden is a haven for birds, and in spring the calls of willow warbler and chiffchaff dominate. Both greater and lesser spotted woodpeckers have bred here, together with tawny owl and willow tit. The ponds are often visited by herons, and especially during the nesting season, by kingfishers. Mammals are also present, but apart from rabbits and grey squirrels, they are seldom seen. From tracks in the snow we know that foxes visit, and there are occasional sightings of stoats, weasels, and hedgehogs. In recent years otters have also been glimpsed. Pipistrelle bats are common, and in some years there is a small breeding group of larger noctule bats. Insect life is plentiful – and on summer evenings somewhat too plentiful! – with several species of dragonfly including the rare Norfolk hawker, and some attractive butterflies, including the comma, white admiral, peacock and brimstone. Occasionally swallowtails find their way to the azaleas from their reed-bed strongholds – adding the finishing touch to the illusion of an exotic environment.

January 2010 in the How Hill Water Gardens.

9 Wildlife Habitats at How Hill

How Hill is often described as 'Broadland in miniature', and most of the main habitats of the Broads can be found here. Reed and Sedge beds, which are cut on a rotational basis to provide the raw material for thatching, are predominant on the western side of the River Ant. The reed harvest takes about three months and starts after Christmas. Saw sedge, a tall strap-like marsh grass, is cut during the summer months and is used for the ridges of thatched roofs. Marsh harriers, water rails, and bearded tits can be found in these marshes, and even the occasional bittern. Bitterns certainly nested in the spring of 2008, apparently the first definite breeding record for decades. There is also a healthy breeding colony of the introduced Chinese water deer. The swallowtail butterfly, on the wing in May and June, lays eggs on the milk parsley, which grows amongst the reeds.

The Brimstone butterfly is always one of the first to to emerge from hibernation in early spring.

Marsh Harrier.

The marsh harrier is the largest bird of prey seen regularly at How Hill, although migrant ospreys are occasionally spotted. Once widespread, the marsh harrier was considered extinct as a breeding species in Britain from 1900 to 1915, and was a very rare bird indeed for most of the first half of the twentieth century. Numbers recovered a little during and after the Second World War, but then plummeted again thanks to the unrestricted use of organo-chlorine pesticides including DDT. In 1971 there was only a single marsh harrier nest in Britain, at Minsmere, but, after this low point, new controls on pesticides brought about a real recovery, and in 1980 there were 20 British nests (Roger Clarke, *The Marsh Harrier*, published in London by Hamlyn, 1995). Their expansion has continued, and they are now seen throughout the year from the How Hill windows. They nest almost every year, usually just to the south of Reedham Water, and their distinctive patrolling flights over the reedbeds can be readily observed from the House. As hunters, they are neither very fast nor very aerobatic, but stealth and perseverance usually help them to maintain a food supply for their own broods, by raids on the chicks of prey species such as black-headed gulls and moorhens. In the winter, the How Hill harriers are assumed to join the celebrated harrier roost at

Horsey at night, and this assumption was proven when a group on our popular Winter Birds Course spotted a female harrier with a singularly distinctive tail on two consecutive days, firstly here and then circling with several other harriers at the roost site. The hen harrier, a species once frequent at How Hill during the winter months, is now much less common in England, and is no longer a regular sight over the Broadland reed beds, although a few individuals still join the marsh harriers at the roost.

Red Admirals are a familiar sight throughout the How Hill gardens in late summer.

The grazing marshes once offered nesting sites for snipe, lapwing, and redshank, but it is now rare to find these birds breeding at How Hill. Flowering plants include marsh violet, tormentil and meadow thistle, but the common rush is very invasive, pushing out other plants. Traditionally, cattle were turned out on the marshes in summer, but groups of ponies are often used to graze these marshes nowadays.

Crome's Broad was first dug out for peat – to be used as fuel – around 1383, and was one of the last true Broads to be created by this process. Water lilies still grow here, and there are some very large pike in the Broad: when left undisturbed it attracts duck, particularly in the winter months, and migrating osprey are sometimes seen here during the autumn.

The Norfolk Hawker dragonfly, a broadland species which has a
stronghold at How Hill, is on the wing in June.

Most of the Dykes or water-filled ditches which criss-cross the marshes were dug out for drainage and for use by reed boats. On the eastern side of the estate, where they are not open directly to the river, they provide a haven for the water plants which are now rare in the Broads themselves, such as water soldier, water violet, frogbit, and stoneworts. The dykes at How Hill abound with small beetles, water boatmen, frogs, toads and newts. The rare Norfolk hawker dragonfly *Aeschna isosceles* is also associated with these dykes, as they provide a freshwater habitat for the larvae: look out for a clear-winged, brown-bodied dragonfly, with striking green eyes, flying only during the month of June. The dykes are man-made in almost all cases, and this is easily confirmed by their geometric pattern. However, the old course of the River Ant is still represented by a long meandering dyke close to the western edge of the estate, giving a hint of what the natural watercourses of the Broads must have been like before they were widened, straightened and deepened to provide the navigable network we know today.

The main dyke of the western part of the How Hill Nature Reserve, showing Yellow Water Lily and true Bulrush (behind the punt).

The dykes on the western side of the River Ant are mostly open to the river, and for many years from the 1960s were subject to the same water quality decline as the Broads generally. In the 1980s these dykes were stagnant and lifeless. However, since the improvement of water quality which followed the suction dredging of Barton Broad at the beginning of the twenty first century, these dykes have enjoyed a resurgence of light, life and colour. The flowers of both white and yellow water lilies, arrowhead and frogbit are now common in these dykes in the summer, and have established themselves from seeds dormant in the mud for years past. Sometimes the dykes furthest from the river are crowded with the beautiful yellow flower spikes of bladderwort, a plant which will only grow in low nutrient conditions, proving conclusively how much cleaner the water has become.

The Woodlands are of two types: the wet carr woodland which develops when marshes are left to themselves, and plantations which were established by E. T. Boardman. Both provide excellent nesting sites for several species of tit, woodpeckers, nuthatches, and woodcock. The gale of October 1987 devastated much of the woodland and several tall pines, oaks and chestnuts, were lost. Woodland areas have been gradually replanted and managed so that there will yet be mature woodland at How Hill in years to come.

Chinese Water Deer.

In 1986, thanks to a grant from the Wolfson Foundation, the Trust created a 'scrape' for wading birds on the wettest part of the Broads Authority's grazing marsh. Two artificial islands were established within this area, and we were delighted when little ringed plovers nested there the following spring, a first for the Ant valley. Later these islands became unsuitable for this species, but avocets have sometimes bred in recent years, and the list of visiting migrants has included pectoral, green, common and wood sandpipers as well as greenshank and garganey. Avocets successfully defend their young against the predations of marsh harriers, but black headed gulls, which have also taken to nesting on the islands, seem to give up their chicks to the harriers without much of a struggle. An early summer vagrant, which hunted dragonflies across the scrape for several days in early June 1992, was a beautiful red footed falcon, which caught and removed the wings of these insects whilst still flying, but settled in the alders at the north east corner to consume the remaining bodies.

A Fox ventures out on to the ice at Crome's Broad, January 2010.

Red Deer forage at How Hill and are occasionally seen on the arable fields next to the lane leading from How Hill towards Catfield.

Foxes are common at How Hill, although seldom seen. Their distinctive tracks can be seen all over the gardens and marshes after snow, and show a fascinating economy of movement: the fox tries always to put its hind leg into the exact print in the snow made by the corresponding front leg. The prevalence of foxes is surprisingly modern: the former gamekeeper Bob Smithson told me that he first spotted one at How Hill in 1960, and told Michael Boardman about it. Michael was very sceptical that a fox should turn up in Broadland, but had to accept the evidence when Bob brought him the carcase. Foxes can swim perfectly well, but they don't generally choose to do so unless forced, and therefore marsh birds have traditionally had a natural defence against predation by foxes. However, there are now several dry access points to the marshes (including metal bridges used for access of machinery) so that this protection has been removed, and fox prints are easy to spot at these access points.

Deer have also increased at How Hill, and three species are regularly encountered. The Chinese water deer, *Hydropotes inermis*, is the most plentiful, and its distinctive 'slots' or hoofprints are everywhere: the cleft hoof splays outwards as an adaptation to life in soft marshy environments. The origin of the population in this country is from escaped animals which came from Woburn Park, and for many years they were regarded as an undesirable alien. Now however, their natural home in China is so badly polluted and developed that the animal is threatened in its homeland, and possibly as much as 25% of the world population is now concentrated in East Anglia. Chinese water deer are often mistaken for muntjac, which have quite recently also been recorded at How Hill, but they are actually quite different, being a much paler and uniform fawn colour. They lack any form of antlers but have large visible tusks, and their ears are packed with dense white fur and are large, rather rounded projections perhaps resembling the ears of well-stuffed toy teddy bears. Red deer pass through the How Hill estate frequently, especially in the winter months, and roe deer are also occasionally spotted.

10 Environmental Science at How Hill

Part of How Hill's uniqueness comes from its commanding position overlooking an important part of the Broadland landscape. The woods, marshes, fens, and expanses of open water which made up Edward Boardman's How Hill Estate are now owned by the Broads Authority. Parts of this area are open to the public, and other areas are kept secluded for the benefit of breeding wildlife. The How Hill Trust is able to make extensive use of this special outdoor resource in our work of inspiring and encouraging children to take an active and enthusiastic interest in the environment. The problems faced by the Broadland environment provide a framework for the study courses provided at How Hill. The central issues are water quality, environmental change and loss of habitat, pressure of tourism and development, and the flooding threat posed by rises in sea level.

The Broads Authority's marshland nature reserve surrounding How Hill is a Site of Special Scientific Interest, and now a National Nature Reserve. It produces an annual crop of reed and sedge for thatching, and provides a habitat for swallowtail butterflies, marsh harriers and other wildlife. The estate includes Crome's Broad, a secluded shallow broad with clear water, which is therefore suitable for the growth of water lilies and other aquatic plants, unlike most of the larger broads.

Testing freshwater for the presence of Nitrates.

Almost every aspect of the Broads is represented at How Hill, and it provides a magical environmental experience for young and old. This experience is underpinned by an introduction to the key environmental issues which confront the modern world.

Dyke Dipping, or more properly, the study of freshwater ecology.

Many of the water quality problems in the Broads result from enrichment by sewage (especially containing phosphates from detergents), agricultural fertilisers, and waste from the large fleet of recreational craft. Increasing acidity in both groundwater and rainfall is also a pressing issue. Upstream from How Hill, the Broads Authority has restored the second largest of the shallow lakes which are the main component of the Broads system. This was the *Clear Water 2000 Project*, involving the removal – by suction dredging – of 300,000 cubic metres of phosphate enriched organic mud to encourage clear water in Barton Broad. How Hill has a significant role in monitoring the success of this project, and a Freshwater Ecology Centre was built here to support public interpretation of this major project. This was How Hill's Millennium project, partly funded by the Millennium Commission and partly by the Broads Authority.

The marshland surrounding the Broads is the result of centuries of management for peat-cutting, reed and sedge harvest, and grazing, and provides a habitat for swallowtail butterflies, marsh harriers and bitterns. The challenge is to find management methods which can maintain these habitats in good heart despite the breakdown of traditional land uses.

Tourism, particularly the boat-hire industry, is still a vitally important part of the regional economy. Tourism is expected to develop along environmentally sustainable lines, so that recreational pressures do not destroy this unique resource. Flooding has always been a problem in such a low lying region, but the threat of salt incursion is now greater than ever as sea levels increase perceptibly along the East Coast. Keeping the sea out of Broadland is the single biggest challenge, and river bank defences are currently being upgraded.

Freshwater Ecology can be engrossing.

The marshes of the How Hill National Nature Reserve provide endless possibilities for Environmental Science projects.

Of course, protecting waterside areas from flooding by raising flood banks is scarcely an adequate response to current threats, and is an entirely inadequate response to climate change. Sea levels are rising, and arguments about the causes of this are still unresolved. Whilst scientists dispute the magnitude and causes of these changes, those responsible for maintenance of existing coastal flood defences are adding alarm and misery to the already hard-pressed residents of low lying parts of East Anglia. In particular, the disgraceful contempt for local residents revealed by DEFRA's Shoreline Management Plan, subsequently adopted in one form or another by all the Councils and Agencies in the region, has demonstrated graphically that the Government is failing in its basic duty to protect life and livelihood in the district. The Broads represent the front line in the war on climate change, and the issues are thrown sharply into focus on a daily basis as water levels fluctuate with every tide and with every shift in atmospheric pressure.

There is no doubt that in due course the Broads will become saline, and eventually they will revert to their prehistoric status as a wide tidal estuary. There are various scientific guesses as to the length of time this change may take, and no doubt any new coastal habitats will have great beauty and natural interest. But the price of all this change will be the loss of an internationally important freshwater wetland system, unique in Britain, not to mention wholesale dislocation of economic and social activity in a densely populated region.

Occasionally, it is suggested that the best way to protect Broadland would be a Tidal Barrier erected close to Yarmouth to keep high tides out of the system entirely. Indeed Edward Thomas Boardman suggested it himself in 1939. During the 1970s the barrier was proposed as a way of increasing agricultural productivity in the Broads, but the idea was eventually sidelined in favour of the programme of river bank works previously mentioned. In any case, the high cost of the proposal, and a concerted campaign by conservationists, (opposed to the inevitable conversion of grazing marshes into arable farmland which would have been needed to make the plan viable) made this a highly controversial issue at the time. The idea has resurfaced in more recent years, with conservationists now ranked in favour of a proposal they once dismissed out of hand. It is almost unimaginable that such an expensive scheme could be implemented now, particularly as it would have to be coupled with strengthened coastal defences if it were to succeed in its mission to keep rising tides out of Broadland.

It is clear that the Broads represent the front line in the war on climate change, but it is tempting to compare the lack of forethought and preparation for this war with the notorious appeasement policy of the 1930s which left Britain so unready for the war with Hitler's Third Reich. A few DEFRA officials seem to think that, if we surrender some of the best parts of the Broads, the North Sea will be content to leave other areas alone! However, local people understand very readily that it is not possible to negotiate with the sea, and that casual abandonment of our defences, even if presented as "Managed Retreat", will scarcely placate the rising tides, and will simply add to pressure on areas currently further inland. Informed management of this problem at a strategic regional level has so far been inadequate, and this issue will be a dominant theme for many years to come.

11 The Swallowtail butterfly at How Hill

How Hill has long been recognised as one of the most reliable places in the Broads district to see the swallowtail butterfly, *Papilio machaon*, on the wing, but in fact this part of the Ant valley system of fens and marshes is not one of the main breeding strongholds of this spectacular insect. Breeding at this site is constrained by the restricted presence of the foodplant, *Peucedanum palustre*, locally known as hog's fennel or milk parsley, by the annual variations in commercial reed and sedge cutting, and to some extent by the availability of nectar sources. The pattern which seems to have emerged in recent springs of warm, dry weather in March and April, followed by cool, wet weather in May and June, which corresponds with the insect's first flight period, must have had a major impact on mating and egg-laying. The season of 2007 recalled the weather conditions experienced in 1987, when April

Swallowtail nectaring from Meadow thistle at How Hill.

temperatures were also very high followed by a gloomy and wet flight period in May and June.

How Hill swallowtails are eagerly anticipated from early May, and the earliest sighting noted in my diary is May 1st (1990), but they continue to emerge here until about the third weekend of June. Early individuals always struggle to find nectar sources, and they are drawn to garden plants such as the red valerian *Centranthus ruber* and even to the deciduous Azaleas in our water gardens. Sweet williams and other cultivated members of the *Dianthus* group exert a powerful attraction for the butterflies. As the season progresses wild nectar sources become more readily available, notably ragged robin, *Lychnis flos-cuculi*, and red campion, *Silene dioica*, and some individuals also attempt to feed from the flowers of yellow flag, *Iris pseudacorus*, although these flowers are deep throated and present quite a challenge.

However, it is not until well into the month of June that the flower which is particularly associated with the How Hill swallowtails really begins to open. The gate opposite to the Broads Authority's information point, Toad Hole Cottage, opens to give access to the Nature Trail, and the first marsh on this trail is easily the best place to find swallowtails. They are attracted by the purple flowers of the meadow thistle, *Cirsium dissectum*, superficially not unlike the familiar knapweed of waysides. Once a common plant of damp lowland meadows, meadow thistle has become much rarer in East Anglia, but careful management has increased the numbers of specimens in this meadow from the original group of three or four spikes which I first recorded twelve years ago. Each year in late autumn or early winter, Broads Authority staff or volunteers have mown at least part of this meadow, and removed the litter, which has encouraged the expansion of this plant, and indeed greater bio-diversity in general. However, winter flooding and grazing by ponies has been effective in creating opportunities for the highly invasive reed, *Phragmites australis*, and soft rush, *Juncus effusus*, and it may not be long before these two dominant species shade out *Cirsium dissectum* and other more sensitive plants. A further complication is that a substantial part of this marsh has been removed to create a new 'soke dyke' as part of the highly damaging Broads Flood Alleviation Scheme, and further invasive work, using earth moving machinery, is scheduled for this area. The declaration of How Hill as a *National Nature Reserve* (15 May 2006) seems to have had only marginal impact on those who have planned and implemented this controversial project.

Swallowtails are often found in the How Hill gardens on sunny days in May and June: Sweet Williams are a magnet for them.

By the middle of June in a typical year there are other plants growing within or alongside the reed fens which provide a valuable nectar source for the adult insects. The common valerian, *Valeriana officinalis*, an erect marsh plant sometimes over one metre tall, with pinkish flowers which rapidly fade to white is not normally very plentiful at How Hill, but sometimes occurs in numbers after a reed fen has been burnt. Still taller is the marsh thistle, *Cirsium palustre*, identified by its spiny-winged hairy stalks, and towards the end of June this becomes the swallowtail's most reliable nectar source. Both these plants grow close to the insect's foodplant, milk parsley, *Peucedanum palustre*, and at this stage of the season there is no need for the butterflies to leave the reed marshes in search of either sustenance or a mate.

However, the search for a specimen of milk parsley has, in recent years, become much more challenging. Dr Brian Wheeler of Sheffield University pointed out to me some years ago that the traditionally neutral or slightly alkaline character of the Broads fens was being compromised by increasing acidity, and the explanation for this subtle but threatening change is highly complex. Precipitation, whether it be in the form of rain, snow or mist, can often be slightly acidic, having been contaminated by atmospheric pollution, which is the result of vehicle emissions or power station discharges, often well to the west of our region. Ground water is also much less pure than once it was, and these changes have undoubtedly led to a decline in those species which need calcareous or neutral conditions. Some species have already disappeared, such as the tall and robust Umbellifer, greater water parsnip, *Sium latifolium*, which is no longer to be found in any of its old sites at How Hill. Others in the same family have become much scarcer, and this includes tubular water dropwort, *Oenanthe fistulosa*, as well as the swallowtail foodplant *P. palustre*. In the summer of 2006 the number of plants of *P. palustre* was so greatly reduced that it was a very simple matter to find the larvae of the swallowtail. Every one of the few plants located had two or more larvae, sometimes as many as six per plant. When the larvae are concentrated on only a few plants, there are obvious consequences. There is increased contact between individuals, resulting in stress and possible transfer of disease. There is increased feeding pressure on the plant, resulting in the decimation of the food source, a particularly significant issue in this case as the later stage larvae eat the leaves, the stalks and even the flowerheads of their foodplant, reducing the prospects for the survival and reproduction of the plant. There is also the probability of increased predation, as the larvae can be more readily picked off by birds: the reed bunting, *Emberiza schoeniclus*, although predominantly a seed eater when adult, feeds its young with these and other species of larvae, and a few concentrations of larvae make easy picking during the nesting season.

Swallowtail caterpillar on milk parsley.

One of Britain's rarest butterflies, the Swallowtail is an icon of the Broads in general, and of How Hill in particular.

There are repeated references in the literature to other foodplants of which swallowtails are said to make use, but at How Hill there are no records of any alternative plants being used for ovipositing. The larvae will certainly feed on other members of the Umbelliferaceae family, and in captivity will readily consume the leaves of the cultivated carrot, *Daucus carota*. The disastrously wet flight season of May and June 2007, coupled with the patent decline in the numbers of plants of *P. palustre*, give very real causes for concern with regard to the future of *Papilio machaon* at How Hill.

In most years there is a small "second brood" of swallowtails which emerges in August. There are never very many individuals seen at this time of the year, and a far greater number remain as chrysalids (pupae) until the following spring. The August females lay their eggs in the normal way, but there is often insufficient time for the caterpillars (larvae) to complete their life cycle before the weather turns cool or wet in September. It is possible that those insects which carry the August hatching gene are in a minority because their ancestors have mostly died out, as a result of the difficulty of completing the life cycle before the first frosts of the autumn, but this has yet to be proven.

Famously, the swallowtail has been known to occur in a black form, in which the markings remain quite visible but the wings are clouded with a black suffusion. Victorian collectors prized this form highly and the marshmen at Ranworth used to supplement their income by obtaining specimens for them. None of these black forms has ever been recorded at How Hill, but on 16th June 2007 I took a group from the Milton Keynes Natural History Society on to the marsh to search for swallowtails, and the first one seen looked somewhat unusual. Several members photographed it, nectaring on meadow thistle, and we were able to study it later, thanks to digital technology. The black markings of a normal swallowtail are fringed with yellow, but on this specimen the black on the hind wings extended completely to the wing margin, and on the fore wings almost so. There was a greater degree of black on the wings generally, and the red spots on the hind wings were reduced. The blue sheen on the hind wings was still present, perhaps a little less so than usual. Other butterfly enthusiasts also saw this insect, and Rob Parker, the Suffolk butterfly recorder, checked the literature and decided that this specimen might be of a rare named aberration called *evita* (Sheldon). If so, it is actually rarer than the black variation, two forms of which have been separately named: *obscura* and *niger*. This unique insect enlivened an otherwise dismal year for swallowtails, which was dominated by cool and exceptionally wet conditions throughout May, June and early July.

Swallowtail variation, 2007.

12 The Marshman's World

Eric Edwards, MBE, was the last of the line at How Hill, the last marshman to be employed on the How Hill estate. When he retired after almost 40 years working the How Hill marshes, at the end of May in 2007, a chapter of Broadland history was closed, presumably forever. The Broads Authority will still undertake work on the marshes, using a combination of conservation staff, volunteers and self-employed reedcutters, but the marshes will never again be looked after in the old established way. Even Eric was unable to carry out the full range of traditional seasonal tasks on the marshes which his predecessors were expected to undertake. However, Eric was pleased to accept a part-time job with the How Hill Trust after his official retirement, and was therefore still able to undertake a certain amount of reed and sedge cutting, and was still able to offer demonstrations of his knowledge and skills. Eric was taught the basic techniques by Bob Smithson, who had been the estate keeper for the Boardman family, so listening to one of Eric's lively presentations about his work at How Hill makes it possible to get a flavour of the lost world of the Broads Marshman. Two themes unify the disparate strands of marsh life. One is the significance of the annual change of the seasons, the patterns and routines of life in harmony with the cycle of the year. The other is the rich harvest of the marshes, the range of natural products and foods which the marshman could gather both for

Reed stacks.

subsistence and sale, giving him and his family a way of life which was undoubtedly more diverse and more rewarding than that of his humble counterpart on the land, the farm labourer.

The life of a marshman in the Broads was harsh but varied. He looked after the drainage windmills, ditches and sluices, and tended the cattle on the marshes. He cut reed, sedge, marsh hay and willow, and he caught eels and fish both for sale and for subsistence. He trapped vermin, and he caught and shot wild duck and other marshland creatures to provide meat for his family's table.

Walter Woolston, in a traditional Broads punt.

Marshmen in the Broads were not all the same. Some owned their cottages and their marshes, but most were tenants: some were employed and some were not. Most were required to look after the drainage windmills, and most were involved with the raising and fattening of marsh cattle. Some had special rights which were really valuable. Bertie High, from Potter Heigham, explained to me how his father looked after High's Mill on the Halvergate marshes, and was

Eric Edwards, Marshman at How Hill for almost 40 years.

able to charge local farmers so much per head of cattle as they were taken past Lockgate Farm, the only route across the marshes to Yarmouth. He recorded these transactions in a wonderful bound ledger which still survives, documenting a truly unique way of life. Until Turf Fen Mill was damaged in the 1912 floods, there were cattle on the marshes at How Hill, and it must have been part of the marshman's life to keep a check on the stock. Of far greater importance here, though, was the harvest of **Marsh Hay**, a mixture of sweet marsh grasses and flowers which was harvested in late May or early June to provide bedding and forage for the horses of urban Britain.

In most years a second marsh hay harvest was possible in July and August, and sometimes even a third crop could be taken (the "aftermath") as late as September. It was a major source of income and a highly organised activity. As with the hay crop in crofting areas, the entire family would be recruited to assist with the harvest, and every patch of land which could be cropped would be included: river banks, dyke edges and the fringes of tracks not excepted. Demand was insatiable at that time in urban England which depended almost entirely on horses for transport, the mix of marsh plants providing the highest possible quality of fodder for the animals. The marshes of North Kent, Essex, Suffolk and Norfolk, the Fens, and even Yorkshire, provided marsh hay on a huge scale, which was transported by wherry and other craft to central storage depots, such as Lockett's Forage Merchants of Horning, before further shipment to the markets. After the First World War, things began to change, as motorised transport developed rapidly, but at How Hill marsh hay was still cropped until the 1930s: this must have been the busiest and most demanding part of the marshman's year. A huge change in the character of the marsh and flood plain landscape resulted after the progressive abandonment of the hay harvest: areas previously kept as wide open treeless expanses of marsh rapidly scrubbed over and the landscape became bushy and eventually wooded. Victorian photographs show wide expanses of grassland and open valleys which must have been windswept and inhospitable in the winter, but which would no doubt provide a marvellous haven for bitterns, harriers and other wild creatures at the same time.

Eric dresses a bunch of reed for the thatcher using a reed rake.

The **Reed Harvest** continues to be an important feature of the How Hill year, although its future is far from certain. Reed can only be cut after the first hard frosts of the winter, which strip away the leaves from the reed stems, and help to wither any other plants which might have grown amongst the reeds. Traditionally, this meant that reed cutting began on Boxing Day and then continued until the new growth of reeds, called the 'colt', started to show through in spring, usually around Good Friday. Cutting the colt would damage next season's crop, but often the reedcutter would continue tying bunches of reed for several weeks after the harvest had been completed. Reed which had been growing for only a single season was always prized for thatching as it would include none of the spindly stalks of previous years: this is 'single wale' reed, as opposed to 'double wale', reed cut after two years, and even 'triple wale', reed left standing over three years. Beyond this reed would have little or no value for thatching, as it would include a good deal of extraneous vegetation in addition to the short reed of previous seasons.

Eric with his scythe.

110

Since the reed harvest was only a winter activity, it could not provide a year round income, and there is some evidence that the Yarmouth fishermen took up reedcutting when it was too cold or too rough to go to sea. Certainly they would have had the thigh length leather boots which would have enabled them to penetrate the marshes, and these might well have proved too expensive for many Broadsmen, as they were bespoke items made to order. A further hint of this maritime tradition is that reed used to be sold in 'fathoms', seven feet round the bonds, equating to a variable number of bundles, which would even out any discrepancies in the size of a bundle. In more recent times reed was sold in long and short hundreds, 110 bunches and 100 bunches respectively. The size of a bunch could be standardised by a measure consisting of a metal strip cut to a half circle and attached to a vertical board, although at How Hill 'three hands and a bit' (the circumference of a bundle at its tightest point) was the recognised measure, and was always seen as very good value. A bunch of reed was one shilling and nine pence (8.75p) in 1969, whereas it sells for around £2.50 today (2011).

The traditional way to carry reed from the marsh.

The marshman's journey to work.

Although old photographs show marshmen cutting reed with a straight handled tool called a **Meag**, which involves cutting the reed by drawing the sharp blade towards the operator, this method has long been superseded at How Hill by the more conventional mowing action of a **Scythe**. A marshman's scythe is shorter than a harvester's scythe, to take account of the unstable marsh surface into which a man would inevitably sink a little, losing some of his natural working height. The skill of reedcutting with a scythe is to mow the reed against the uncut growth, so that it stands up even after it is cut, obviating the need to scrabble around in the wet mud to gather the crop. This is assisted by a curved wand of hazel wrapped around the shaft of the scythe, called a **boil**, which steers the reed towards the standing crop, particularly with the assistance of a small reversible peg affixed at the widest point of the boil, which Eric Edwards calls a **pricker**. In reality, nowadays most reedcutters use machinery for the harvest, which speeds up the process but does not necessarily reduce the element of hard work involved. Machines developed for rice harvesting are often used, but they are cumbersome and difficult to manoeuvre in the marsh. In any case the reed still has to be dressed and bundled by hand, and this is a time consuming and skilled job.

Tools of the marshman's trade.

The **Meag** remains useful for cutting the roots of weeds growing in dykes, which then float upwards and can be removed using a **Crome**, a long handled right angled fork. The vegetation along the edges of dykes is trimmed with a **Shore Knife**, usually a farmer's hay knife straightened by the local blacksmith. Shallow foot drains which let water into or out of a marsh are dug out using a heart shaped spade or **Hodder**, and the mud can be scooped out from these ditches using a **Slubber** or **Mud Scoop**. Deeper water can be dredged using a **Dydle**, which has an iron ring mounted on a very long handle, netted to catch the mud and with a sharp leading edge to cut through clumps of vegetation. In earlier times, marsh dykes were cleared out regularly using these wonderful old tools: sometimes it was necessary three times a year, and every winter a major clean out, called "**bottom-fying**" – getting right to the bottom of the dyke – was undertaken. No doubt my grandmother, when she referred to "fying" out a cupboard, was using a politer version of the same word. Few dykes in the Broads are maintained to this standard now, but mechanical diggers are used when and where the landowner can afford the expense.

The **Sedge Harvest** is undertaken from May to October, when the plant is still growing and when it is green. It then needs a period of two to five years for re-growth. *Cladium mariscus* or saw sedge, also known as the great fen sedge, is a tall strap-like marsh grass with sharply serrated edges to its leaves, which produces large brown florets in late summer. At present it is rare for sedge seeds to germinate to create new plants, for reasons which are little understood, but the plant can increase by vegetative means. A typical bunch of sedge will include a variety of other grasses and other flowering plants, including reed, but most thatchers prefer this mixture as it is easier to use and offers fewer sharp edges. Sedge plants can be killed if water covers their crowns too soon after harvest, and careless management can reduce a sedge bed to a desolate mudflat: unlike reed beds, they can also be easily damaged by insensitive use of machinery. There are a number of other species of sedge many of which were cut in the past as a component of marsh hay or to be scattered on cottage floors. At present sedge is not imported into the UK but it grows extensively in Eastern Europe, where until recently it was used for bedding and forage for farm horses.

In the Broads sedge grows almost entirely in those areas which were dug for peat in the nineteenth and early twentieth centuries, and it has become relatively rare in the rest of Britain. Sedge beds are marshes of great biodiversity, with plants such as greater spearwort and marsh helleborine often appearing amongst the sedge plants. Birds such as reed buntings often make their nests in sedge beds, and although as adults these birds are strictly vegetarian seed-eaters, they feed their young on the great abundance of insects which occur in this rich habitat.

The sedge harvest.

A freshly harvested bunch of sedge is flexible and, when folded tightly over the ridge or apex of a thatched roof, will make an attractive and weatherproof capping. Sedge used in this way does not last as long as the reed thatch which it caps, but will need replacement every 15 or 20 years. The earliest documented reference to saw sedge as a roofing material is apparently given as 1926, but this is plainly absurd since How Hill itself was ridged with sedge in 1904. In any case it is unimaginable that such a material would not have been used in earlier times, as cottages were generally thatched with whatever was to hand: grass, heather, bracken and turf have all been used. Such dwellings would not have looked pretty by modern standards, and might have been shared unintentionally with a host of wildlife, but their roofs kept out the worst of the weather. In the Netherlands the use of sedge as a thatching material is unknown – roofs were capped using a linear roll of reed bundles locking into one another, or more recently with a series of bright orange tiles, with an inverted v cross section, laid over the ridge.

In the past there were other harvests from the marshy flood plains of the Broads district. One such was the true **Bulrush**, also known as common club rush, *Schoenoplectus lacustris* (previously known as *Scirpus lacustris*). It should be distinguished from greater reed mace, which many people confusingly call bulrush. The true rush grows in deep water, including dykes, rivers and lakes. The plant is now rare in the Broads, although there has recently been some evidence of recovery. The stems of this plant are large and tall, often growing to a height of up to three metres, and seven or eight centimetres in circumference. The brown florets are borne at the tip of the stalks, in clear distinction from many other common species of rush. The plants appear to respond well to an annual cut, below the water surface, which seems to stimulate next year's growth.

There is still a rush harvest each summer in the east midlands of England. Felicity Irons spends the summer months of June, July and August harvesting bulrush on the River Great Ouse in Bedfordshire, Cambridgeshire, the Nene in Northamptonshire and on the Avon River in Warwickshire. She continues a tradition formerly concentrated on the Ouse going back many centuries. The bulrush is cut from long punts with a rush knife, a slim scythe-shaped blade one metre long fixed to a two-metre handle, enabling the rush stems to be cut from the river bed. Each day's cut is transported to a drying field and fanned out on stubble to allow sun and wind to dry the rush over a few days.

During the drying process the weight of the rush is reduced to a fifth of the fresh rush and while the rush will withstand limited showers, prolonged rain will rot and destroy the stems. The variation in weather during this process naturally produces extraordinary and beautiful shades of colour – prolonged sun bleaching the rush to yellows and mellow browns while overcast periods mean the rush holds more of the original intense green and produces muted pinks, gold and purple. There is no chemical treatment of the rush at any point during the harvest or in the weaving of the final designs. Once dry, the bulrush is graded into size and tied into 'bolts' or bundles of approximately 2.5 kilogrammes on the field or hedges before being stored in a thirteenth century timber framed barn close by.

The true bulrush has long been used for the making of mats and large baskets, such as log baskets. The rushes are flattened and then woven by a simple process rather like plaiting of long hair. The resultant woven strands are then stitched together to produce long lasting and durable soft furnishings. Traditionally bulrush has been used in the manufacture of chairs, and a wide range of other products even including hats. Bulrush is no longer harvested commercially in East Anglia, but the Waveney Rush Growers, now based at Oulton Broad, still produces high quality floorings amongst other products. Other species of rush have also been harvested in the past, and one well-known and common use for the peeled stems of soft rush was to make low grade lamp wicks.

Marsh Hay, How Hill Staithe, 1929.

Willow must once have been a hugely important crop in the Broads area but there is surprisingly little published information on the subject. There are many hundreds of species and types of willows, which are all deciduous trees which belong to the family Salicaceae. Those willows which are traditionally used for basket making and for hurdle fencing are grown in those wet marshland areas which have alkaline soils, where they are sometimes known as osier beds. Although this has ceased in the Broads, two main species are still grown commercially in Somerset: the Black Maul or Almond Leaved Willow (*Salix triandra*) and the Common Osier or Basket Willow (*Salix viminalis*).

Wherry, How Hill Staithe, 1935.

Willows were, and in Somerset still are, planted in willow beds, some 16,000 plants to an acre, each bed lasting between 30 and 40 years. Each willow sends up shoots two to three metres tall. Harvesting begins in October when the last leaves have fallen from the stems and continues through the bleak, wet, winter months until April. Harvesting was once back-breaking work with a hand-hook which was used well into living memory, and many local willow-growing families remember punting the cut willows out from the soggy moors in flat-bottomed boats along the wide drainage ditches, known in Sedgemoor and the other Somerset Level as 'rhines'. The withies are tied into bundles and taken to the yard where they are sorted into various lengths – from one to three metres. They can be processed to provide various colours: some are used as they are, the bark being a deep green colour; a portion of the harvest is stood in a shallow pit of water which causes the sap to rise and the withies to leaf again allowing the bark to be stripped away revealing the white wood beneath. Most are boiled for a day to make stripping easier, this also stains the wood a gingery brown colour due to the natural pigment within the bark, this is known as buff and is the most popular material for baskets. Traditional basketmakers need to work with stripped willow and, until the willow stripping machine arrived between the two world wars, willow stripping was entirely done by hand, with each stem pulled individually through a hand 'brake'.

Toad Hole Cottage, no longer a marshman's home, 1920s.

As the 19th century ended there were hundreds of willow growers, willow merchants, basketmakers and furniture makers throughout lowland England. They supplied the London hotel and catering trades, the fishing industry, factories in the industrial North, the Post Office, and butchers, bakers, farmers and fruit growers. Baskets were standardised, and the 1916 British Amalgamated Union listed precise measurements and quantities of willow for many items, including hawkers' baskets, plate baskets, scuttles, wool skeps, and linen baskets, as well as pheasant hampers, bread trays, sieves, pickers, cycle crates, homing pigeon baskets and even coffins and bath chairs! Willows are still used extensively for a wide range of basketry items as well as fencing hurdles, but sadly the harvest has virtually disappeared in East Anglia.

For most of the Broads marshmen their main activity was looking after the cattle grazing on the marshes, and tending to the Drainage Windmills which kept the summer pastures dry enough for grazing. Early photographs show cattle on the marshes behind Turf Fen Mill, which is now an extensive reedbed. Cattle were grazed on the Clayrack marshes until recent years, but the enormous problems faced by livestock farmers have meant that this traditional aspect of the Broadland scene is also now in serious decline. In my early years at How Hill, in the 1980s, days were frequently enlivened by chasing a cow out of the camping field back onto the grazing marsh, wild west style, and even this is now but a distant memory.

Toad Hole Cottage.

A much loved feature of the How Hill estate is Toad Hole Cottage. This traditional marshman's cottage is built of hand-made bricks fired in a kiln at How Hill. There was a cottage on this site in 1740 but the present one is probably early nineteenth century. The last occupant was Ben Curtis, a marshman and eelcatcher who operated an 'eel-sett'. This was a large funnel shaped net stretched across the river at night to catch the migrating eels, which were then kept alive in an underwater eel trunk.

The cottage has two bedrooms with sloping ceilings tucked underneath the thatch: they are approached by a set of 'Norfolk winders' (stairs) from the living room. Water was originally taken from the river, and later a hand pump was installed outside the cottage. Toad Hole was partly restored in 1956 and again in 1986: it is now managed as a small Museum and Information Centre by the Broads Authority.

Toad Hole Cottage.

Toad Hole Cottage, December 2009.

13 Drainage Windmills at How Hill

There are three drainage windmills, all of different designs, at How Hill. Boardman's Mill and Clayrack Mill are accessible from the footpath beside the River Ant, and Turf Fen Mill is to be seen on the opposite bank. All three are consigned to the care of the body formerly known as the Norfolk Windmills Trust, now called the Norfolk Mills and Pumps Trust.

Turf Fen Drainage Windmill.

Turf Fen Mill was built by millwright William Rust in about 1875 and is typical of the brick tower mills of Broadland. It has a Norfolk boat-shaped cap, six-bladed fantail and four double-shuttered sails of seven bays each. An unusual feature is the double scoop wheel with a choice of high or low gears. It was used to drain the area now known as

'Reedham Marshes' but it was damaged in the 1912 floods and eventually stopped working early in 1932, when the marsh was no longer to be used for cattle. The original builders were highly proficient: they must have buried a great deal of material in the marsh (perhaps tightly bundled faggots) before they started to build the heavy inward sloping brick walls. Even so the structure developed a slight lean away from the river towards the marsh, and noting this they were able to correct for this effect as they laid each subsequent course of bricks, so that the top of the mill is, even now, perfectly true. The Norfolk Windmills Trust took over responsibility for Turf Fen in 1976, and by 1986 major restoration work was complete, including a new cap and sails. The late Norfolk millwright John Lawn of Caston did most of the work, and he would be dismayed to see its currently neglected state.

Turf Fen Drainage Windmill.

Boardman's Mill, also known as the Skeleton Mill, was built in about 1897 by Daniel England, the Ludham millwright and engineer. It is an open timber trestle mill with an eight-bladed fantail and four double-shuttered sails, each with six bays. England's drawings show the mill driving a scoop wheel and this was how it was originally constructed. It was improved in 1912, following the floods and finally, in about 1927, the present turbine was installed, making Boardman's Mill unique. The mill stopped working in 1938 when it was blown over in a gale. It was

Boardman's Mill.

restored by Richard Seago for the Norfolk Windmills Trust during 1979 to 1981, and has had various maintenance works carried out since.

The hollow post mill, now known as **Clayrack Mill**, started life on the marshes at Ranworth (on the River Bure) in the middle of the last century, but by 1903 it was disused and decaying. The mill was 'rescued' by the Norfolk Windmills Trust in 1981, but restoration work was seen as a threat to wildlife on the site at Ranworth, so the mill was re-sited

Clayrack Mill.

on the Clayrack Marshes at How Hill. Restoration work was finished in 1988 and the machinery was also restored, so for a few years the mill could actually be used to demonstrate how the Clayrack Marshes were drained. Sadly in recent years this mill has been subject to serious decay and is now in need of extensive renovations.

Clayrack Mill.

14 The How Hill 'Hitler Oak'

There is an oak tree in the grounds of How Hill House which, at first glance, could simply be any other oak tree. This tree, however, is remarkable, as one of only two out of 130 'Hitler Oaks', as they were named, believed still to thrive on British soil. These trees were presented to all gold medallists at the 1936 Berlin Olympic Games. The How Hill oak grew from a sapling awarded to the British gold medal-winning

Lalage.

Six-Metre Yacht class crew, skippered by Christopher Boardman, whose father Edward Thomas Boardman founded the How Hill Estate at the start of the twentieth century.

More than 70 years after the infamous Games, 'Hitler Oaks' crept back into the national conscience in August 2007 when one of only four oaks won by Britons at the Berlin Games became the second of the British trees to be felled. The 50 foot tree, donated to Hendon School following former pupil Harold Whitlock's Berlin victory in the 50 kilometre walk, succumbed to a fungal disease and was felled to prevent injury to children. Only a year earlier a letter to the *Daily Telegraph* Sports pages noted that another oak, awarded to rower Jack Beresford and planted at Bedford School, had also been removed in order to build a sports hall although the school's biology department took cuttings and planted them throughout the school estate. The demise of the Hendon and Bedford trees meant there were potentially only two acorns of Olympic history still flourishing somewhere in Britain – those trees won by the Six Metre sailors and by the 4 x 400 metre relay team, accepted by runner Godfrey Rampling, father of actress Charlotte.

Arguably the most famous athlete to participate at the Berlin Games was the American sprinter Jesse Owens, whose historic four gold medals are commemorated alongside one of his trees proudly standing in the grounds of James Rhodes High School, Cleveland, Ohio. However although helming the British boat, *Lalage*, to overall victory at the Olympic regatta, which took place at Kiel Bay in the far north of Germany, Christopher Boardman did not himself attend the medal ceremony. I recall that Chris didn't really agree with how the yacht racers were treated at the 1936 Games. They were a long way from Berlin and didn't really feel a part of everything. He told me that they didn't win a single race, and won the gold medal because of an unusual handicapping system in use at the Games.

Chris sailed to gold with *Lalage* owner Charles Leaf and their crew of Miles Bellville, Russell Harmer and Leonard Martin, the team taking the title by one point from Norway, who had themselves actually won three races to Britain's zero during the course of the regatta. Nevertheless, despite his apparent disquiet with events in Germany, he retained the sapling and it was planted in a low key ceremony on the family property where its magic is enhanced with every passing year. One of the stories Chris used to enjoy telling is that on his return to England, he disembarked the ferry at Harwich and went straight to a pawnbrokers to see what he could get for his gold medal, only to discover it was not in fact made of gold but base metal! Chris repeated this story for the Anglia TV cameras when the How Hill Boardman Room was officially dedicated to the family, but Peter Boardman, President of the Friends of How Hill and Christopher's nephew, remarked: "I like to think that he was joking when he told that story!" Christopher left his gold medal, on his death in 1987, to the National Maritime Museum in Greenwich.

Planting "Hitler's Oak" at How Hill.

Twice events have conspired to eliminate How Hill's oak from the scene. Hitler himself was inadvertently almost responsible for its demise during the war when a returning German bomber randomly dropped two bombs in the How Hill neighbourhood and shrapnel hit the rear of the house. It was nature's turn to do its worst in the Great Storm of 1987 when the tree was damaged by the gales but saved by neat tree surgery.

Hitler's Oak, How Hill, January 2008.

Sailing was Christopher Boardman's passion throughout his life and as well as his Olympic feats, he was also hugely proud of his role in Sir Thomas Sopwith's 1934 America's Cup campaign on board *Endeavour*. He was part of the crew which took the *Endeavour* to sea after Sopwith's professional crew went on strike for more pay! *Endeavour* was considered to be the best yacht of her day in the J Class, and was nearly 130 feet long overall. At the America's Cup races in 1934, she came very close to defeating the American defender *Rainbow*, and set for the first time in the history of the Cup, a double-clewed jib, which had been designed by her owner, who was also the skipper. While she was tuning-up in the Solent, however, astute American observers had spotted her novel jib in time for the defender to be equipped with a similar type of sail. The tense atmosphere was heightened by the feeling that the Americans had behaved badly, and at least one of the races ended acrimoniously with a disputed finish. Sopwith was furious, claiming for many years that he had been cheated out of his deserved victory.

During the Second World War, Chris was a Corvette Commander in the Atlantic. Following his father Edward's death, as the eldest of five children he inherited the House and grounds at How Hill, but he could not afford the upkeep of the property and reluctantly sold it to Norfolk County Council in 1967. Having moved to Cornwall after marrying Elaine, Chris returned to his native Norfolk in the later years of his life.

When presented, the young oak sapling was accompanied by a message bearing the legend "GROW TO THE HONOUR OF THE VICTOR". It is to be hoped that Christopher's story, and the memories of all those who did Britain proud with their sporting endeavours at the Berlin Games, will live on as long as the 'Hitler Oak' continues to live its unremarkable life in the car park behind How Hill House.

15 Reflections on How Hill
by Michael Boardman

Michael Boardman, the youngest son of Edward Thomas Boardman, often reminisced about his happy years living at How Hill. He frequently recalled his many forays into the marshes, and painted an idyllic picture of life at How Hill. Lying in bed in his room (now room 14), his early mornings were often enlivened by the haunting and eerie calls of bitterns and other denizens of the marshes. He was asked if he would kindly contribute to the Newsletter sent regularly to the members of the Friends of How Hill, and the following two essays were the result.

1. First published in January 1991.

I have been asked to write a few notes about incidents which happened whilst my family lived at How Hill. I must admit at once that I do not pretend to be either an ornithological or plant expert but, except for the war years I lived there from about 1919 until 1966. Nevertheless I did not take an immense interest in natural history in so far as it existed in the area which was part of Broadland – the River Ant running through the estate and Crome's Broad hidden away amongst the trees.

During the last war my father constructed an air raid shelter in the hill a few yards from the house on the river side. I do not think it was ever used although a bomb did fall and explode within about fifty yards from the house on the north side and I understand some windows were broken and another fell on a marsh leaving a large crater. After the war ended something, probably a rat, had made a hole adjoining the shelter at the top and one year a pair of kingfishers made a nest in it. The eggs hatched and both the parents used to bring small fish to feed them. They always carried them lengthwise in their beaks presumably to eliminate wind resistance. I had a wonderful view of these beautiful birds from my bedroom window which I shall never forget. Occasionally I used to walk down to the river after dark. Near the staithe the soak dyke which runs parallel with the river was very narrow with high banks on both sides. There was a small bush growing well below the top of this on which a kingfisher roosted regularly, no doubt it found shelter from the wind there. I used to light it up with a torch to see it asleep with its little head, or maybe just beak, tucked under its wing. Not wishing to disturb it I only lit it up for a second.

On one occasion a nightingale spent a few days in the water garden amongst the azaleas. I had heard it was there so one night, about 11 p.m. I went to listen to it singing. Although it was too dark to see it I got very near and heard its wonderful song several times. Some distance away across the river three bitterns were booming in different areas. There were no other sounds except the odd quack of a duck. I found this a wonderful and rare experience hearing two such different birds singing at the same time although it is questionable whether you can call the booming of a bittern singing! Unfortunately it is a long time now since I heard a bittern boom as they are extremely scarce now. They starve of course in prolonged hard winters.

Michael mending a fishing net in his bedroom at How Hill.

At one period two marshmen were employed. Between December and the middle of April they cut the reed which was sold for thatching. In the summer they cut the sedge which is used for the ridging at the top of a house in thatching because it is pliable. One of these marshmen, George Saul, was at one time a fisherman in the North Sea. I was very grateful to him for teaching me various knots and how to mend nets. An uncle had already taught me how to make them. For many years bow nets have been set on the Broads to catch fish, in fact one of Emerson's photographs, at the beginning of this century, shows these nets being set. They are in the shape of a cylinder about a yard long and two feet high. The two ends narrow in towards the middle so that fish, once in, cannot find their way out and ruin the net or at least make a very large hole. I made six of these nets so could block the average ditch completely. You can set them singly along the edge of banks but they are no good in open water. I really only used the nets occasionally in order to find out what fish were about. I set them in at night and looked at them the following morning. The fish were never hurt and none the worse for spending a few hours in their prison. It was extremely exciting pulling up a net shaking with tench and bream. The best tench I caught on the broad weighed just over four pounds, but the biggest was on the Bistley marshes which weighed just over five pounds. I was pleasantly surprised catching such a big one but it swam away quite happily.

Michael Boardman settling into a shooting butt, Bistley Marshes, 1936.

The marshmen of course did other jobs such as cutting the yew hedge which took about a fortnight in August. It was all done by shears as hedge trimmers had not been invented. On wet days they cut up firewood for the house. After the reed cutting finished in April they tidied up the garden for opening to the public at the end of May and early June. They were wonderful workmen and no-one ever knew them to do a job badly.

Michael Boardman with a young bittern, May 1923.

With regard to wild plants there was the Osmunda or royal fern which grows quite tall and is very impressive. My father used to move some into the water gardens where they became numerous. Sometimes there was grass of parnassus, if the conditions were right for it – a very pretty delicate looking white flower. Also the crested fern which I believe is not common. There was a lot of bog myrtle, the flowers of which go a golden colour and give off a pleasant and strong scent. There was a lot of milk parsley, the only plant which the caterpillars of the swallowtail butterfly feed. We used to collect these caterpillars and my mother fed them on milk parsley until they turned into chrysalids when they were put into special boxes lined with perforated zinc to let the air in, but hopefully nothing else. The ensuing butterflies were released when they hatched. Unfortunately not all did hatch and we did not know the reason so asked the late Ted Ellis about it. He always seemed to know the answer to every natural history question and he told us that those failing to hatch would have been destroyed by the parasitic ichneumon fly. He advised us to try find the caterpillars when they were black and still small because it was likely at that stage this parasite would not have become attached. This was more easily said than done as the small black caterpillars were far harder to spot than the larger green ones.

One of my favourite birds is the bearded tit. These were quite numerous and allowed a fairly close approach. They follow the reed cutters around on the look out for insects which the men disturb. They seem to like to make their nest in thick sedge.

If the above article turns out to be of some interest, there are of course other topics and incidents which on some future occasion I could either remember or extract from diaries kept by me over rather a lot of years!

2. First published in June 1991.

I have been asked to write a further article for the Newsletter relating to life at How Hill whilst I lived there.

I think my earliest recollection as a child is going down to the River Ant to watch a trading wherry being unloaded at the staithe. The wherry had brought furniture etc. from Norwich when we moved permanently to How Hill. I distinctly remember a large dolls house coming out of the hold. One must remember that in those days (I cannot remember the exact year) there was not much transport for moving the contents of a house. I suppose there was no great hurry so it was decided to move at least some of the things by river. How they were moved to the wherry from the Norwich house I do not know, but they went from the river to the house at How Hill by cart drawn by a donkey. Of course the donkey had to make several journeys and I was told that on one of them something rattled a lot which frightened the donkey so it "took off" leaving behind whoever was leading it. Somehow it was traced and captured in the next village of Catfield.

A shooting party, 1937. From left to right: Michael Boardman, Humphrey Boardman, Jack Williams, Chris Boardman, Meredith Perrin, Bob Smithson.

From a fairly early age I became interested in ornamental ducks and my father let me keep some in the Bog Garden, which was enclosed with wire netting. He agreed with me that being in full plumage in winter and early spring they provided colour which the plants did not do then. He got quite fond of a pochard drake which used to follow him about. However understandably he objected to keeping too many as they nibbled the banks away and exposed the roots of the shrubs. The tree ducks were the most colourful, especially Mandarins and Carolinas. These in the wild state would only nest in trees with holes in them but having no trees with suitable holes artificial nesting boxes had to be dotted about with boards running up to them. These ducks have a sharp claw at the back of each leg which enables them to climb vertically. One Carolina was always escaping from the garden up a post holding the wire netting. It was going to a nest it had made outside. One Rosybill drake lived there for 14 years before it died.

Across the river in a westerly direction from the house and on the South of Reedham marsh were some grazing marshes known as Bistley. Lying below river level they were drained by a windmill standing next to the River Ant. About 1932 this windmill broke down and the owner did not think it worthwhile repairing it. Also to set the sails a marsh man had to come a long way from the village of Irstead. Fairly soon these marshes became permanently flooded the water rising and falling in accordance with the level of the river.

It was as if a new broad (admittedly a shallow one) had suddenly appeared. It soon became a paradise for birds and fish. Except for the original drainage ditches you could walk about in thigh waders or use boats with shallow draughts: of course it greatly improved the view from the house. These marshes were bought about 1945, I think. The adjoining reed bed of about 20 acres always held a booming bittern and presumably a nest. Bearded tits nested in the sedge lying along the edge of the old ditches. Herons loved it because it was easy for them to catch a fish in the shallow water. I once counted 17 there at once. We used a powerful telescope to see what birds were about. If a harrier appeared, which was quite frequently, any ducks which had been sitting around on islands flew around and landed on the water knowing that harriers normally kill their prey only on land. However I did once see a harrier keep picking up a damaged coot off the water and dropping it but I do not know how this saga ended. On another occasion I saw 5 different species of duck in the field of the telescope without moving it. Apart from mallard, clutches of the ducklings of shoveler, teal, gadwall and tufted duck were seen at times. On the river there was once a pochard with 7 ducklings.

When I was an early teenager I had to earn pocket money by destroying rats, mice and sparrows. Poisons such as are used nowadays had not then been invented. We used to keep chickens and lost a lot of food through these pests. The things killed were entered in a note book. I think it was 6d per rat and 3d a sparrow. Periodically my mother paid me the amount owing. Being a hoarder I still have this note book somewhere. Two mongrel dogs called "Fidget" (brown) and "Smudge" (black) used to help with the rats and mice. One Christmas both these dogs disappeared which was very worrying. Somehow we got them back to find they had been on the rampage. Some man came and asked my father if he was the owner of two dogs one of which was black and the other brown. He had to admit ownership and it transpired that the pair had gone hunting and killed 5 turkeys and about 12 chickens belonging to this man. Presumably this happened at night when the free range birds had gone to bed in a chicken house. It would seem that one dog had driven them out and the other killed them as they emerged through a door. I think they were found dead outside. I remember seeing them all laid out. Father of course apologised for these murders and paid the compensation asked, the man letting him keep the birds to eat as there was nothing wrong with them. These dogs were marvellous ratters but rather overdid things on this occasion.

Turf Fen Mill, sunset, November.

Picture Credits and Acknowledgements

The old photographs reproduced in this book are mostly from the Boardman family albums, started by Mrs Florence Boardman and lovingly augmented by her sons, especially Humphrey. I am grateful to Peter Boardman, Mrs Shirley Place and Mrs Pauline Boardman for their help in securing these photographs. Some of the other old photographs are from my collection. Peter also provided the picture of Prince Charles meeting local children on page 63.

I am immensely grateful to my very talented niece Hannah Broom for the drawings and for the map.

I am hugely grateful to Steve Routledge, of Barnetby-Le-Wold, Lincolnshire, for some superb wildlife photographs: Swallowtail, Norfolk Hawker and Brimstone (pages 86, 89, 100, 104 and rear cover). I recommend anyone interested in Natural History to look at Steve's beautifully illustrated Wildlife Blog, at **www.juncea.blogspot.com/**

Mike Page, famous for wonderful aerial photographs of East Anglia, kindly allowed me to reproduce his very striking shot of How Hill from the air (page 4). Other dramatic examples are to be seen at **www.norfolkskyview.flyer.co.uk/**

The Chinese Water Deer, whilst often seen at How Hill, is difficult to photograph, and I am delighted that Robin Chittenden allowed me to use his image from **www.robinchittenden.co.uk** (page 91).

The photograph of a Marsh Harrier (page 87), another very challenging subject, was taken by the superb Turkish photographer Akif Aykurt, to whom I offer my sincere thanks.

The professional photographer Richard Denyer has often visited How Hill, particularly to record some of the many high profile visits organised by the Broads Authority during the enterprising years of the 1980s and 1990s, and I am truly grateful to him for the picture of Prince Charles at our front door (page 63). His work is sure to inspire and to fire the imagination: visit **www.richarddenyer.co.uk/**

In recent years most of our celebratory events have been captured on camera by Anna Meek, ARPS, APAGB, and I have relied on her to provide magical shots of some key events at How Hill (pages 67, 71 and 73). I am so grateful to her for her support over many years.

The photograph of "the author in his natural habitat", at the helm of the electric boat *The Alderman Norman*, on Barton Broad, (page 144) was taken by another long-term supporter, Jean Bobbin: again I am very grateful for her assistance.

The rest of the photographs are mine or from my collection. If I have inadvertently used a photograph without acknowledgement, I am sorry for the oversight.

On patrol, Barton Broad.

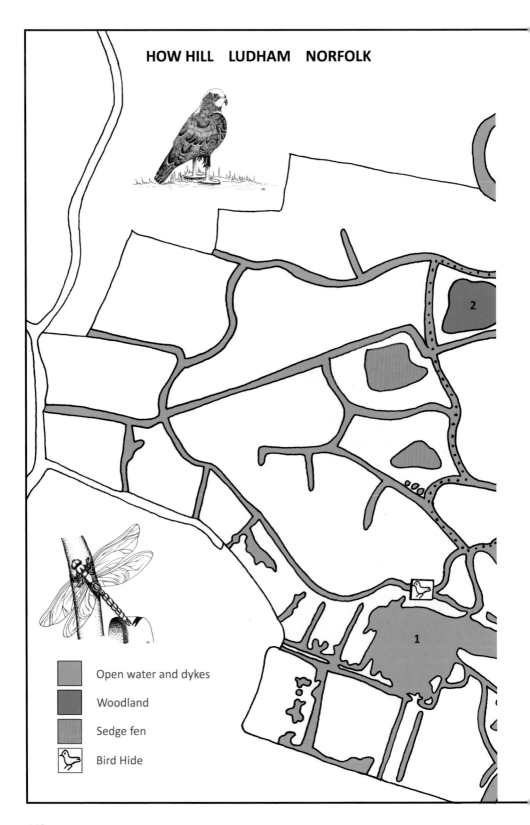

HOW HILL   LUDHAM   NORFOLK

Open water and dykes

Woodland

Sedge fen

Bird Hide

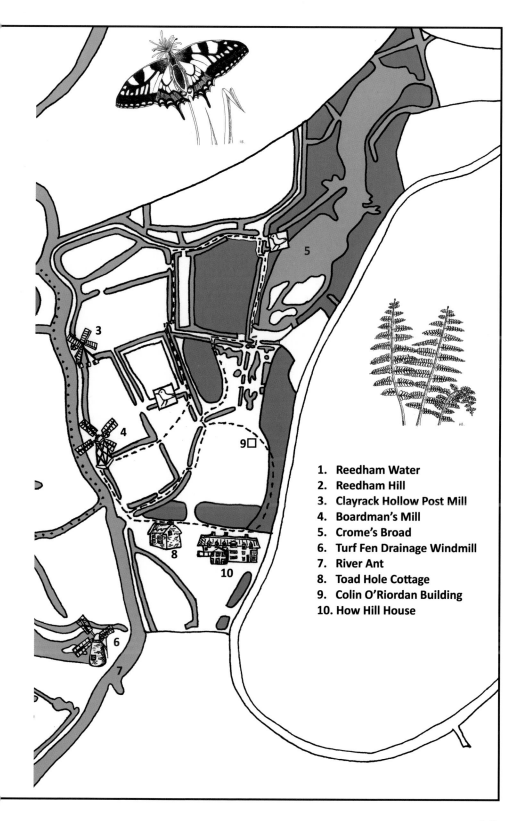

1. Reedham Water
2. Reedham Hill
3. Clayrack Hollow Post Mill
4. Boardman's Mill
5. Crome's Broad
6. Turf Fen Drainage Windmill
7. River Ant
8. Toad Hole Cottage
9. Colin O'Riordan Building
10. How Hill House

The view from How Hill, December, 2009.

The author, David Holmes, MBE.

How Hill Water Gardens, May 2009.

How Hill Water Gardens, December 2009.

Sunset, Turf Fen Mill,
January 2011.